Custom Bicycles

A passionate pursuit

REVISED EDITION

Custom Bicycles

A passionate pursuit
REVISED EDITION

By Christine Elliott
and David Jablonka

Foreword by Phil Liggett

images
Publishing

Published in Australia in 2012 by

The Images Publishing Group Pty Ltd

ABN 89 059 734 431

6 Bastow Place, Mulgrave, Victoria 3170, Australia

Tel: +61 3 9561 5544 Fax: +61 3 9561 4860

books@imagespublishing.com

www.imagespublishing.com

National Library of Australia Cataloguing-in-Publication entry:

Author:	Elliott, Christine.
Title:	Custom bicycles : a passionate pursuit (revised edition)
ISBN:	9781864704945
Subjects:	Bicycles–Customizing.
	Bicycles–Design and Construction.
	Bicycles–Pictorial Works.
	Skilled labor.

Other Authors/Contributors: Jablonka, David.

Dewey Number: 629

Edited by Driss Fatih

Designed by The Graphic Image Studio Pty Ltd, Mulgrave, Australia

www.tgis.com.au

Pre-publishing services and printed by Paramount Printing Company Limited in Hong Kong on 128gsm Chinese Matt Art

Contents

6   Foreword by Phil Liggett

8   Introduction

12   Anderson Custom Bicycles

16   Baum Cycles

24   Bilenky Cycle Works

28   Black Sheep Bikes

34   Bob Brown Cycles

38   Bohemian Bicycles

42   Bruce Gordon Cycles

48   Calfee Design

56   Columbine Cycle Works

60   Crisp Titanium

66   Cycles Alex Singer

70   Cyfac

76   Davidson Handbuilt Bicycles

80   Donhou Bicycles

86   Don Walker Cycles

92   GURU Bikes

98   Independent Fabrication

104 Ira Ryan Cycles

110 Jeff Jones Custom Bicycles

118 Keith Anderson Cycles

122 Kirk Frameworks

128 Kish Fabrication

134 Llewellyn Custom Bicycles

140 Lynskey Performance Designs

146 Marschall Framework

152 Moots

158 Naked Bicycles and Design

162 Pegoretti

170 Richard Sachs Cycles

176 Roark Custom Titanium Bicycles

182 Robin Mather

190 Signal Cycles

198 Steve Potts Bicycles

206 Strawberry

210 Sweetpea Bicycles

214 Vanilla Bicycles

220 Vendetta Cycles

224 Vicious Cycles

228 Wolfhound Cycles

236 Contact details

238 Photography credits

240 Acknowledgments

Foreword

A bicycle frame-builder is no ordinary man. He is a craftsman, an engineer, an artist, and a perfectionist, who through his extraordinary talent has produced a machine that can carry man over the highest mountains, along the narrowest roads, and over huge distances. He has given man the ability to travel under his own power at speeds in excess of 100 kilometers per hour on a machine that seems as flimsy as a balsa wood toy, yet in reality is as strong as a Centurion tank.

For more than 150 years—since Scotsman Kirkpatrick Macmillan produced a bicycle with pedals from his smithy in Courthill, Dumfrieshire—we have seen this machine evolve. Even today it continues to change its shape, wandering away from the traditional diamond frame, as these unique frame-builders use modern materials in their search for more speed.

One finger is all that is required to lift a modern-day bicycle built from the lightest components known to man—a far cry from the 52-kilogram quadricycle built for Prince Albert, the husband of Queen Victoria, in the 19th century.

However, this beautiful coffee-table book is not about the history of the bicycle, but instead focuses on some of the specialist frame-builders who from their bases around the world produce, to this day, the finest bicycles ever made. Often constructed in ridiculously small workshops in the backstreets of cities around the world with little more than a blowtorch and a vision, these sleek works of art—because that is what these bicycles are—roll into the full view of the public without ever receiving the fanfare they deserve.

Many of these great modern-day artisans are listed in this book with their work bared for all to see and scrutinize. From places as far apart as New York and Norwich or Geelong and Grants Pass, Oregon, the pages here reveal the finest bicycles of our time. Machines designed to carry you to the shops or over the highest road in the Pyrenees—the Col du Tourmalet—are awaiting your awe.

Having raced for 12 years and reported on the Tour de France for more than 40, to me there is nothing kinder to the eye than a bicycle. Throughout my life, it has carried me (not always as fast as I would have liked!) far and wide and never complained. If you can make the journey, it certainly can.

A friend of mine passed an exceptional milestone by accomplishing his 1.6 millionth kilometer in a lifetime spent logging every kilometer ridden since a boy. He was even late for a dinner we had arranged for him in his honor because he was circling the venue until that special landmark was reached.

You will love browsing through this book, even if you have little or no interest in cycling. These thoroughbreds live in their own special stable, having been produced by special people; so admire and envy their work, as they can do something that very few people in the world can do: build a bicycle.

Phil Liggett
Hertford, United Kingdom

Introduction

We are most excited to present an updated edition of *Custom Bicycles: a passionate Pursuit* that features many new images and revised text to keep you up-to-date with the creative output of our featured builders. The work presents a selection of the many frame-builders around the world who dedicate their lives to designing and creating beautiful, handcrafted bespoke bicycles. Each chapter visually showcases their craftsmanship with illustrations of their bikes and unique features, while the accompanying text tells of the personal journeys that inspired each designer to become a custom bicycle frame-builder. The chapters offer personal insights into how their skills were developed and also feature the philosophy behind the techniques used and choice of building materials.

The featured builders range from highly experienced master builders, who have many years and hours of frame-building underpinning their expertise, through to those who represent the next generation of visionary frame builders. All the frame-builders in this book have been motivated by the ambition to create bikes in their own special way, while taking inspiration from traditional designs and more

experienced builders. *Custom Bicycles: a passionate Pursuit* is by no means a definitive representation of custom bicycle builders, but a colourful snapshot of some of the leading manufactures at work today.

In a consumer-driven world where many things have a use-by date, owning a handcrafted bicycle that has been custom-fitted to suit your body and riding requirements is an investment in quality and longevity and has the potential to become a family

heirloom. These bikes are not only practical, human-powered machines, but works of art that make you want to throw away your car keys and go riding down a road or along a trail in search of the sense of freedom that is reminiscent of flying through the air.

Whether these bikes are referred to as bespoke, custom-made, or hand-built, the rider is always at the centre of the design, and every frame-builder has their own technique for measuring and assessing

each customer. The time taken to build a bike depends very much on the size of the business, and design complexities. Many of the builders are lone craftsmen or work in a team of just two and are able to execute every stage of the process through to the finished product. There are also the builders who gather a small to medium team of people together, each with a particular area of expertise. Then there are the larger companies that are able to maintain the personal, hand-built nature of a bespoke bicycle.

When it comes to preference of materials such as steel, titanium, aluminum, carbon fiber, or more exotic materials such as bamboo, they are chosen for their particular characteristics, design abilities, and intrinsic riding qualities. A bespoke bicycle can be made in any style, depending on the performance needs of the customer. Some builders specialize, but most build a range of bicycles and collaborate with the customer to develop their dream bike.

Whether a customer wants a road or track bike for racing, a mountain bike for exploring, a city bike for commuting or running errands, a touring bike to see the world, or a long-distance bike for randonneuring, obtaining a bespoke bicycle will take any rider on an exciting journey with a talented artisan who has the ability to put them on the road in great comfort and style.

Christine Elliott and David Jablonka

Anderson Custom Bicycles

St. Paul, Minnesota, USA

Dave Anderson loves dropouts. Not for counterculture reasons, but from the point of view of a bicycle builder. His favorite feature on a bike happens to be dropouts, particularly when they are stainless, compact, smooth, and elegant. Making custom bikes seemed to be a natural path for Dave to follow, as he had always enjoyed making things from a very young age and he really loved bikes. Dave builds his custom bikes from both steel and carbon; however, the majority of his bikes are made from steel because he finds that it is ideally suited to making custom frames and feels that it's the only material that really allows the builder to put his "mark" on his work: "I use the materials that I feel are best for a given situation. To a certain extent, form follows function, and both form and function are heavily influenced by how I want the bike to look and perform."

Dave describes himself as a "jack-of-all-trades" and when it comes to building bikes, he is a one-man shop involved in every step of the building and finishing process. Depending on the complexity of a bike design, it can take anywhere from one to two or more weeks to complete a bike. If he is building a fairly basic design, it could take him a week, including the painting. When it comes to a more complex design, where there is considerable carving, detail, polished stainless steel, and lots of graphics, it can take an experienced frame builder like Dave Anderson two or more weeks to complete a customer's dream custom bicycle.

Believing that everyone can benefit from owning a custom-made bike, his philosophy is reflected in these words: "A truly handmade custom bike is designed and built for you and you alone. It will fit you perfectly and will be built with materials and components that reflect you and your riding style. A good custom bike will also say a lot about you, your personal tastes, and your sense of style." With every customer, Dave is literally building a bike from the ground up to fit their body, riding style, and the purpose for which it will be used.

"A truly handmade custom bike is designed and built for you and you alone. It will fit you perfectly and will be built with materials and components that reflect you and your riding style. A good custom bike will also say a lot about you, your personal tastes, and your sense of style."

"I use the materials that I feel are best for a given situation. To a certain extent, form follows function, and both form and function are heavily influenced by how I want the bike to look and perform."

Full stainless steel frame with polished lugs and stays

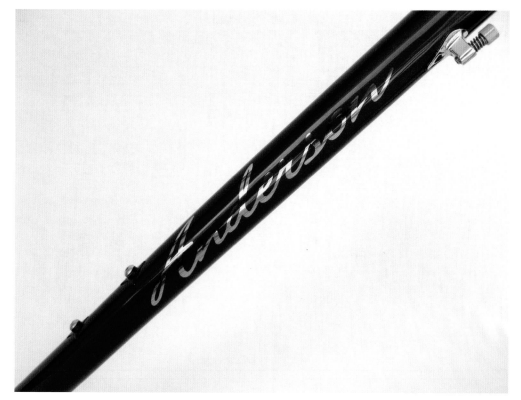

It looks fast standing still …

"I've wanted this bike for the last ten years and it was well worth the wait. I worked closely with Dave on every aspect of it. The end result is a bike that not only looks fast standing still, but one that also fits my body, personality, and riding style perfectly. Beauty is only skin-deep, but this bike must be ridden hard to appreciate why I love it so much. Balance is the best way to describe it. When I grit my teeth and start swinging from side to side, it responds like no other bike I've ever ridden—and I've ridden a lot of bikes. The bike rides so well that I do not hesitate to take it on 5-hour-plus rides."

Guy Stone

Lugged Reynolds 953 stainless steel frame set

Baum Cycles

Geelong, Victoria, Australia

Darren Baum's family tell a story of him as a baby lying in a bassinet in his father's workshop and instinctively knowing to turn away as his father struck an arc. When Darren became old enough, the mechanic who worked for his father became his mentor and taught him welding, machining, and fabricating. Darren spent every night, weekend, and holiday period plus any spare moment working for him, until he eventually started working in a bike shop. At age 14, Darren Baum's first foray into bike-building was a tandem built out of tubing from his father's workshop, constructed so that he and his mate could ride together in the Great Victorian Bike Ride.

It was in 1989, while Darren was still at school, that he had his first real taste of life as a frame-builder. He organized two weeks of work experience with master frame-builder Brian Cross and was sponsored with a Reynolds tube set. Darren was eager and keen to build his first real bike, but Brian had other ideas and was not going to let him anywhere near his tube set until he had first learnt a few essential basics. On his first day, Darren was kicked out of the workshop and told to walk around the block to have a good

hard think about why he didn't have any grease on his seat post. On his return, he had to learn how to file and was given a painted tube with several layers of different colored paint. Using a particular filing technique, Darren had to learn to file off each layer without touching the next colour. By early afternoon he had proven he could do it and said to his boss, "Can I build my bike now?" To which Brian replied, "No, now you need to learn to do it left-handed."

The hand and construction skills that Darren gained in his early years gave him an incredible jump-start into his aircraft maintenance engineering apprenticeship. During this period, Darren extended his skills by learning how to do computations from the engineers and completed further welding training at night school. He is now regarded as one of the best welders in the business: "When I sit down to weld, I know exactly what the hand movements are going to be for the next 30 seconds, where I'm moving to, and where I'm going to stop." Darren finds the best time to do welding is early in the morning before the rest of the Baum team arrive, because it's very relaxing and he also likes to hear what he's doing.

Darren's single objective, right from the beginning, was to gather the skills to become a bicycle frame-builder and in 1996 the first Baum frame was sold commercially. Darren likes to make the sort of bikes that he enjoys riding, which is why he uses titanium and steel to construct his bikes. The Baum Cycles approach to the art of bike-building is to create an integrated holistic design. In line with this philosophy, and in order to maintain complete control over the processes, all Baum Cycles facilities are housed under one roof in the coastal town of Geelong. When designing a bike for a customer, the most important thing to consider is what the true end use is going to be. This may range from racing, touring, riding on a bike path, or weekend racing to the café.

All Baum bike frames are named after different types of coffees, in recognition of the changing dynamics of the riding set, which these days is more likely to be riding to a café than actually training to race. "Espresso coffee, you're there, you drink it, you get on your bike. The Espresso frame is the same—it delivers exactly what you want."

"When I sit down to weld, I know exactly what the hand movements are going to be for the next 30 seconds, where I'm moving to, and where I'm going to stop."

Darren Baum welding a titanium frame

Darren Baum stamping the serial number on a titanium dropout

I love the brushed titanium …

"I love the brushed titanium finish and my friends are in awe of the cool workmanship on joints and cutouts. As for the ride, well it's exceptionally comfortable and easy on my commute to work—it takes all those bumps and ramps on the cycle track with ease. We've spun along Beach Road, and in the top gears it's fast and smooth. I can't wait to load the panniers and head out on a multi-day trip, where I expect it to come into its own …"

Derarca O'Mahony

Darren Baum, founder of Baum Cycles sitting in front of a titanium-framed Cubano

Romano tourer, with a brushed titanium finish

Steel-framed Espresso

"Espresso coffee, you're there, you drink it, you get on your bike. The Espresso frame is the same—it delivers exactly what you want."

Bilenky Cycle Works

Philadelphia, Pennsylvania, USA

Stephen Bilenky's career tinkering with machinery began at the age of three, with a percolator coffee pot. He sat on the floor taking it apart and putting it back together. This gave him the confidence to disassemble Sturmey-Archer gear hubs a few years later. His childhood playtime was consumed by building and modifying model trains, cars, treehouses and bikes. He started a bike repair shop in his garage aged 10—an expansion of his comic book and penny candy store which was already up and running. "I did all the bike repairs in a radius of three blocks. That's when I realized I was a mechanical entrepreneur."

He landed his first bike shop job at Supreme Cycles, Philadelphia in 1965. After school, weekends, and vacations were spent working in the shop and he gradually moved up to become manager of the shop. He also worked as a bike mechanic in State College, Pennsylvania, while studying agriculture at Penn State University, from which he graduated in 1975. He opened Bike Doctor, a repairs-only shop, in Philadelphia in 1977, transforming it into a boutique shop in 1982. All this was the career path into framebuilding: "Building your own frames is a bike shop owner's PhD.", says Bilenky. He launched

Sterling Cycles as a brand in 1983; the name was changed to Bilenky Cycle Works in 1992.

Bilenky Cycle Works is a happy, dirty place that turns out exquisite, clean machines to suit the needs of riders of every size, shape, and desire. Ranging from pieces of "rideable jewelry" to utilitarian workhorses, each frame testifies to Bilenky's pursuit of aesthetic functionality. All models are produced by Steve and his dedicated team of craftsmen. Working at Bilenky isn't a job— it's a calling.

In his scant off-hours, Steve plays bass guitar alongside fellow original members of the late '70s band, the Notekillers. The discovery in 2003 that they had been a formative influence on SonicYouth (and by extension, the entire noise-rock revolution), caused the Notekillers to re-form after a hiatus of more than 20 years. The subsequent contact with Sonic Youth's Thurston Moore led to the re-release of the Notekillers' old recordings on Mr. Moore's own Ecstatic Peace label. New recordings and numerous gigs across the country soon followed, as well as an appearance at the All Tomorrow's Parties festival in England in 2006, and a European tour.

The "FrameBuilder's Express" party train to NAHBS 2008 was one of the latest additions to the fun and adventure that makes up the world of Bilenky Cycle Works. They take an active part in the Philadelphia cycling community. Each December they host a cyclocross race in the neighboring junkyard—the only junkyard 'cross in the world. Riders clamber through vans, ride through schoolbusses, brave giant see-saws, and avoid toxic mud. The crew thinks all the racers are insane, but hundreds show up every year.

In 2010 Bilenky produced the inaugural Philadelphia Bike Expo. With dozens of exhibitors, classes, rides, races, seminars, and thousands of visitors, it was a huge success. The 2011 Expo built on the popularity of the first, and the event is quickly becoming a beloved Philadelphia tradition.

Rides like a dream …

"Now that I've been riding my Bilenky for about six months (my daily commute and a couple of short tours have somehow totaled almost 3,000 miles), I can wholeheartedly say that I'm really happy with the bike. The mix of components we worked out together has been very reliable and cost-effective. The bike itself is not only beautiful but rides like a dream—of my three bikes it's certainly the most-ridden. I love how versatile this bike is and, unlike my other two bikes, I'm sure I'll still be riding my Bilenky 10 years from now, if not longer. Yeah, the bike cost me some money, but when you think about how long I'm going to have it, I think it's actually working out to be a really good deal."

Thomas Delaney

Artisan Tourlite—753 tubing with stainless-steel lugs

Bina Bilenky's 26-inch-wheel Tourlite

Show frames from Cirque du Cyclisma 2007

Stephen fillet brazing dropouts

Fork finishing

Black Sheep Bikes

Fort Collins, Colorado, USA

Black Sheep Bikes comprises the collective craftsmanship, design, and creativity of James Bleakley, Todd Heath, and Paul Knowles. Their quest for building bicycles comes from a driving passion to create something that evokes the feeling they had riding bikes when they were teenagers. The aesthetically pleasing curves of the 1920s, '30s and '40s have inspired Black Sheep to incorporate them into their designs. Adapting contemporary geometry, materials, and fabrication techniques allows for the lines of the past to become the bicycles of today.

The Ivor Johnsons, some Schwinn designs, a number of bikes that were built pre-World War II in the USA—where curves first started to appear in the cantilever style—twin top tubes, and S-bent down tubes have all inspired Black Sheep Bike designs. Although the most efficient way to connect two points is with a straight line, James believes that when another step-like curving tube is added to the design, it creates complexity: "the other benefit you get from a curve is compliance. When you're trying to compress a straight line that doesn't necessarily want to bend, if you introduce a curve, it

automatically creates a way for some compliance in the design." This allows for a frame or fork to be very light and handle well, while providing a nice comfortable ride.

Black Sheep Bikes wants to build bicycles that last a lifetime—something a customer can leave in their will. Building a custom bike for someone takes into account many measurements, including height, inseam, torso, and arm length. The end result is designed to work in unison with the user's body. James explains: "many people can find it hard to find a bike that fits them well off the rack, especially women. What they are often trying is a small man's bike, and women's proportions can be very different."

Black Sheep Bikes builds a number of models where the top tube has a negative curve to accommodate greater standover and ease in mounting and dismounting. Consideration is also given to where and how the individual is going to ride, the length of ride, the shape of the bike, and, of course, the size. These are also often customers' dream bikes—no

small detail can be overlooked. Light mounts, racks, bottle openers, and internal routings are all options. If you can imagine it, Black Sheep wants to build it for you.

Despite their busy schedule—customers currently have to wait more than a year for their order—the guys at Black Sheep Bikes still make time to go out and ride the bikes they build. Their personal feedback is what helps develop the bikes for the future. "We are really building the bikes we want to ride," says Todd with a smile: "riding our bikes is what keeps us motivated and reminds us why we love what we do." Their cycling ranges from a casual Thursday night ride to Single Speed World Championships, or to James' seventh attempt at the Leadville Trail 100 in Colorado. Racing creates a space where they have dedicated time to ride, while staying connected to the community of riders who race and ride Black Sheep Bikes. Once they return home you find the three friends back in the shop listening to music, turning out the next customer's dream bike.

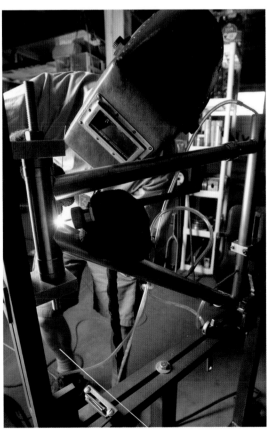

"When you're trying to compress a straight line that doesn't necessarily want to bend, if you introduce a curve, it automatically creates a way for some compliance in the design."

Bob Brown Cycles

Saint Paul, Minnesota, USA

The smooth, fluid lines of nature have provided inspiration for Bob Brown's lug carving and shoreline shapes during his custom bike building over the past decade. With nature supplying an infinite source of structures and shapes, Bob has far more ideas for designs than time will ever allow him to complete. Bob Brown builds exclusively with steel and stainless steel and likes to combine the classic look of a lugged frame with today's modern materials. His full stainless-steel frames are a great example of a traditional style executed with a very modern material.

Like many custom bike builders, Bob performs every aspect of the frame construction and design all the way though to the paint and assembly of a complete bike. Being a solo worker suits Bob because when he's building a frame, so much of what is executed relies on the vision he has in his head. He describes himself as a tool junkie and his workspace is filled with a vast array of machinery and equipment, including some 50- to 60-year-old tools that were handed down from his grandfather. However, even with all the modern implements in the world he maintains that his most important tools are still his vise and files. Bob spends a lot of time hand-filing

each lug to create just the right curve or shape: "I put a lot of love into those parts and I think it shows in the final product."

The advantage of painting his own frames also allows Bob to design certain features of the frame to be painted in a specific way, creating a truly unique end product. An example of this is when he shapes stainless steel lugs to ensure nice natural boundaries where the paint will stop at the lug edge or partway on the lug. Bob's favorite part of the whole building process is without a doubt brazing the frame: "I don't know why, but I love executing a really clean braze on a complicated part. Finishing off a braze with just the right amount of filler so that there are no voids and just a perfectly crisp lug shoreline is really rewarding."

When Bob isn't shaping, polishing, or painting a customer's unique frame, he's out riding bikes or cross-country skiing. He tries to run as many errands as possible on his bike each day to keep active, satisfied that there's one less car on the road. He's also a sucker for ultra-endurance activity, so he tends to do a lot of really long rides, runs, and skiing sessions.

Bob loves to share his passions with others and has been known to coach high school ski teams for fun during the winter season. If you're out enjoying some local music in Saint Paul, Minnesota, you may also spot Bob playing drums in a local band called Derailleur, which has been another lifelong activity. Bob Brown likes to do anything but sit still.

Dragonfly lug with copper-plated finish

"I don't know why, but I love executing a really clean braze on a complicated part. Finishing off a braze with just the right amount of filler so that there are no voids and just a perfectly crisp lug shoreline is really rewarding."

Complete sport-touring road bike

Polished stainless-steel lugged bicycle

"I put a lot of love into those parts and I think it shows in the final product."

Seat lug detail, polished stainless steel lug

My bike was built to change my life ...

"Because my bike was built for me, it looks exactly like I want it to, handles exactly like I had always hoped a bike would, and, literally, has saved my life. Bikes may be just bikes to some, but not to me. My bike was built to change my life. Starting back in late 2005, weighing 501 pounds, I had only one way out ... or else I'd be dead. My way out was to ride a bike that was built for me. I'm currently down to 219 pounds—my bike has saved my life. In the process, my bike gave me more freedom, enjoyment, interaction, insight, and revelation than nearly any other single thing in my lifetime. If those aren't all great reasons to love your bike, I sincerely don't know what is. Bob Brown built my bike, and I ride that bike every single day."

Scott Cutshall

Brazing a fork in the jig

Bohemian Bicycles

Tucson, Arizona, USA

Dave Bohm knew from a very early age that he wanted to design some kind of transport; he was car and motorcycle crazy and after discovering bicycles he realised that, at the time, they were much more accessible to him. Dave believes that bikes are much more than a machine—they are also art in a usable format. He considers himself very fortunate to have been exposed to paintings, sculptures, buildings, and automobiles at a very young age and holds the belief that his handcrafted bicycles are objects truly created from his mind as well as his hands.

The type of material from which a bike is made is inconsequential to Dave because he believes great bicycles can be made from a multitude of materials such as bamboo, metals, or carbons. The most important thing to him is how particular materials are utilized and how they either allow or inhibit creativity in design and form. For various reasons he has chosen to work exclusively in steel for its almost unlimited design flexibility and because it's a very forgiving medium. Composite materials promise the same type of freedom, but Dave feels that working with steel best utilizes his skills: "There are many excellent bicycles made from other materials, but in this area I

excel, so I stick with it." Dave works alone mostly, but has recently taken on an apprentice helper who frees up his time to concentrate on the more detailed and creative work, which is the hallmark of Bohemian Bicycles.

Unlike many other frame-builders, Dave's background is in precious metal as a silversmith, and so he brings a skill-set to his work that is rarely seen in the industry. While first and foremost the bicycles must perform the task for which they've been designed, Dave considers detailing as the icing on the cake and enjoys the lug preparation and paint stages the most: "To that end I incorporate nontraditional lug-cutting, accoutrement in precious metals, original stainless dropouts, nameplates, themes, and paint that are all completed to the highest caliber."

Many of Dave's customers have been riders for some time and through interviews and the reviewing of various pictures and designs, they come up with a riding position and design together. Apart from the usual measurements, fitness level, flexibility, and intended riding purpose are all extremely important factors in the fitting process. A large number of Dave's customers have become good

friends and continue to email him with their travel stories and pictures of their Bohemian bikes.

One of the most rewarding aspects of his business is that each customer brings a unique purpose to the bike-building process. For example, Dave was given the opportunity to design and construct a unique tricycle for Noel Kreidler, who has muscular dystrophy: "Noel has limited use of her lower limbs so the cycling motion was something she could do to maintain lower body strength. Her old tricycle was extremely heavy and had limited gears; the design of her new trike enables her to tackle hills as well as cruising on the flat. It features a very low standover height with a wide, open mounting platform that enables her to mount the trike much more easily. I'm glad Noel gave me the opportunity to be creative and find a solution that will keep her healthier, longer."

Recently Dave has been passing on his expertise by running a frame-building course. The 10-day workshop, which covers everything from design and fitting to welding, brazing, and paintwork, offers cycling enthusiasts the chance to craft their own frame under Dave's watchful eye. He has gone one step further with some clients, instructing them how to build a bike from scratch.

Rohloff touring bike frame

"I incorporate non-traditional lug-cutting, accoutrement in precious metals, original stainless dropouts, nameplates, themes, and paint that are all completed to the highest caliber."

Bohemian Orange Crush 29nr

My trusted companion …

"I never considered taking any bike but my faithful Bohemian to the Pyrenees. Dave builds beautiful and functional bikes, and mine had been my trusted companion for over 55,000 miles, including the Cochise Classic 250, the Death Ride, several bike tours of Colorado and El tours, and about 100 trips up (and down) Mt. Lemmon in Tucson, Arizona. The bike is comfortable on long rides, steady as a rock on descents, and no other bike would do for a once-in-a-lifetime trip like the Pyrenean Raid—more than 400 miles of epic climbs in four days."

Rupert Laumann

This tricycle was custom-built for Noel Kreidler

Bruce Gordon Cycles

Petaluma, California, USA

Bruce Gordon is a highly regarded master frame builder who has been crafting bicycles since 1976. Bruce has a similar background to many other experienced bike builders—he worked in a bike shop at a young age, was into cycling, and got hooked on the idea of making his own bikes. The bicycle that Bruce Gordon is particularly known for is his touring bike, which is deemed by many touring aficionados in the United States as one of the best touring bikes around. Today, the vast majority of Bruce's work consists of TIG-welded steel touring bikes, although his real creative expression is evident in his steel-lugged bikes, which he built for the first 12 years of his building career. Bruce has returned to building these bikes because of the depth of detail and creative expression that can be achieved.

The traditions of frame building and levels of craftsmanship are evident when ordering a custom-made bike from a frame builder with as much experience and expertise as Bruce Gordon. His skill levels are such that he has built a one-off, lugged-titanium bike that nobody else would come near to producing. As much of Bruce's reputation is built on his touring bikes, particularly his Rock 'n Road model, many people seek him out to get their dream touring bike constructed for that special trip that they've been intending to make for years. Many of Bruce's customers range from people in their 70s who want to tour the world, through to younger riders who are discovering a love for touring.

When designing a touring bike for somebody, it's imperative to Bruce that there is appropriate geometry, tubing, and well-positioned rack mounts that cater to the specific purpose of touring bikes. His aim is to figure out how he can make a bike for touring that will function better than anything else that is out on the road or currently available. In recent years, Bruce has been turning his design skills toward many innovative ideas and has created new custom bike part designs out of titanium. The designs are reminiscent of the French style and his range of aesthetically crafted accessories include front and rear panniers, racks, CNC'd milled rear lights and cantilever brakes, toe clips, pumps, and seat posts. Bruce Gordon is always trying to stretch the design boundaries with his bicycles in order to create a point of difference.

Calfee Design

La Selva Beach, California, USA

Well before mountain bikes were invented, Craig Calfee was one of those kids who took his regular bike into the woods, and in doing so joined a generation of young trailblazers who helped to create the concept of mountain bikes. During his college years, Craig graduated to riding bikes in New York City as a bike messenger, and when his bike was damaged he discovered an interest in its structure. Although he was an arts student majoring in sculpture, it was at this point that Craig began to think about bikes as industrial design.

At the time, he was working at a carbon-fiber boat building company and used the materials he was working with and his own techniques to build himself a new bike. This first bike didn't fit him very well, so he decided to learn more about the technical aspects of bike construction. By borrowing a friend's Massachusetts Institute of Technology library card, Craig read everything he could get his hands on and sought out advice from other frame-builders. He then moved to California and began building carbon-fiber frames in his San Francisco garage. Three-time Tour de France winner Greg LeMond discovered Craig's

bikes in 1991. The thrill of seeing Greg wearing the yellow jersey, riding a bike that he had made, provided the inspiration for Craig to delve deeper into the possibilities of bicycle design.

Craig had always been interested in trying out new things and playing with unorthodox materials, and in 1998 he started building bikes out of bamboo for family and friends. His bamboo bikes were such a success that in 2006 Calfee Design began producing them for the general public. Craig believes bamboo offers even more opportunities to customize than carbon fiber because the bamboo tubes allow for an infinite variety of naturally formed diameters and wall thicknesses with which to work. Bamboo also provides natural butting because the cane grows a thick wall at its base and the wall thickness tapers as it grows. Calfee bike designs are very much embedded in nature and the notion that form follows function.

Calfee Design has also extended its bamboo bike-building philosophy and skills to help people in Africa construct bicycles. Many years ago, Craig traveled through Africa and learned that bamboo was a plentiful resource and that people were very creative and skilled with their hands. In June 2007 he went to Ghana on a feasibility study funded by the Earth Institute to investigate the viability of local production of bamboo bikes. As it turned out, there was keen interest in projects that are self-sustaining and add value to communities' skills and economies. Craig regularly returns to Ghana to continue helping the community develop their skills. Back in California, the 32-member team at Calfee is fortunate to work in a beautiful beachside location near Santa Cruz, where there is plenty of good light and ventilation with views of agricultural fields. "You really can't ask for a better location. It's very aesthetically pleasing and close to nature."

Columbine Cycle Works

Mendocino, California, USA

Established in 1979, Columbine Cycle Works had its genesis in the childhood years of the Murphy brothers. John and Richard were making and fixing things such as bikes and soapbox cars, and were fed a steady diet of powered model airplanes, boats, and cars from as early as they can remember. Light racing bikes became their next area of interest, inspired by Richard's job at a Denver pro bike shop in the early 1970s. This sparked an interest in frame building and by 1979 they registered the name Columbine after a period of time building, repairing, and repainting frames.

Establishing Columbine was a natural progression for John and Richard as they have always shared the same core value that bicycle making epitomizes: that simplicity and beauty can elevate a simple machine to an art form. "It is a complete passion with social, athletic, technical, and aesthetic dimensions." A hallmark of John and Richard's frame building has always been to try to find a way to build the lightest frames available. They believe the weight of a frame is the fundamental ingredient

in making a first-rate riding bike, and that comfort and longer life expectancy are engineered by controlling the spring-like movement of the tubes. John's background in structural physics has allowed him to assimilate those ideas while developing the lightweight methodology. He prefers to work with steel or stainless steel because both metals have a very good modulus of elasticity, along with other specific properties with which to build the perfect unbreakable spring. According to John, "Steel makes bikes that 'sing' to you!"

There are many features on a bike that John Murphy admires, but he's particularly fascinated by the sparkle of a really light set of stainless tension-spoked wheels on a running bike, which he describes as a mechanical marvel that's nothing short of miraculous. When it comes to frame features, he usually finds himself checking out the seat stay cluster for geometric delights, or there's always the well-crafted rear dropout joint for its expression of creativity.

Columbine bikes are well known for the intricate accoutrements, elegant lugs, and paintwork that adorn them, elevating them to moving works of art. Although they build bikes that provide a metal canvas for exquisite creative expression, the philosophy and challenge that really underpin John and Richard Murphy's ultimate goal is to make ultra-light frames that will ride like a dream.

"It is a complete passion with social, athletic, technical, and aesthetic dimensions."

Crisp Titanium

Arezzo, Italy

Darren Mark Crisp can still describe his first two-wheeler bike in great detail. Those two wheels gave him a sense of freedom and movement, but the future bike builder was already wanting to trim the seat stays back to make his AMF Roadmaster look more like the slick Schwinn Scrambler BMX bikes that all the cool neighborhood kids were riding. For a boy who grew up in the United States, there seems to be a certain synergy and logical progression to how Darren finally ended up designing and building bikes in Italy out of his material of choice, titanium.

His take on bike design was very much influenced by seven years of project management work in the construction industry. Overseeing the building of exclusive, high-end retail stores from materials such as stainless steel, nickel steel, nickel silver, and titanium gave Darren the opportunity to use some of the finest tooling equipment, do lots of welding, and liaise with the top engineering and fabrication minds alongside elite designers and architects. This period of his life very much influenced his take on bicycle design and his approach to building—clean lines, no frills, form follows function, high-tech—as well as his desire to build a better product.

When Darren first started building bikes, he was using True Temper steel and Henry James lugs for much of his work, though he also experimented with other materials such as aluminum and scandium. In 2001 he attended the United Bicycle Institute to study titanium frame design, which effectively sealed the deal on his choice of metal for bicycle frame building. Darren's studio is located in Tuscany, where he lives with his family in a villa surrounded by vineyards, olive groves, and a scenic view of the walled town of Castiglion Fiorentino. While music usually provides a relaxing backdrop to Darren's working day, in spring and summer he prefers the comforting sounds of live music provided by the *merli* (blackbirds) in the early evening and the sound of his family talking and playing in the adjacent yard.

Darren performs all the design development, cutting, welding, and finishing work. Welding, however, is his favorite part of the building process, which he finds particularly stimulating for various reasons: the challenge of laying the perfect bead, the rhythm that is both relaxing and exciting, the technical aspects of the sterile weld, and the mechanics of fusing titanium tubes together and looking at a freshly

finished welded frame knowing that it's only days away from being on a road or trail in some faraway place. Aside from the overall form and design of a bike, which is his first priority, he likes dropouts because they are very revealing. They can divulge where the builder is from, the design intent behind the bike, and the taste of the cyclist: "I don't think there is any one aspect of a frame that tells more of a story than the drops."

His decision to work exclusively with titanium is strongly based on his experience in the metals industry and from learning early on that making the best products requires having complete understanding of your building materials. Darren chose titanium because of his direct working experience, along with its magnificent ride qualities. He believes it is a superb material for building bike frames because it is corrosion-resistant, provides a supple ride, is lightweight, and has the mechanical strength needed to build a frame for a lifetime: "You can update components on a yearly basis, but the elegant look of a custom titanium frame is timeless."

Head tube/fork detail

Apart from the sheer beauty ...

"I think the most gratifying aspect of a custom-made frame is the knowledge that it has been made for me. Not some standardized model of me, but the real me with all the physical quirks nature has given me. If you add titanium into the equation, with all its durability, ride quality, and so on, then you are getting close to perfection. While there are plenty of gorgeous bikes out there (and I have no objection to carbon fiber itself), now I've got a bike that rides great and is going to last forever, and I actually know the guy who created it. Hard to beat."

Brendan Jones, Rome, Italy

Crisp custom titanium road bike

Crisp custom titanium 29er

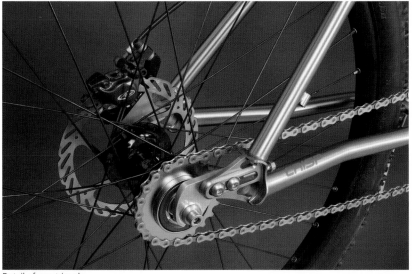
Detail of rear triangle

Seat tube/top tube detail

Crisp demonstrates welding types

Tacking fixture

"I don't think there is any one aspect of a frame that tells more of a story than the drops."

Amadeo Bonfanti competing on a Crisp

Veneto champion Dionisi heads toward victory

"You can update components on a yearly basis, but the elegant look of a custom titanium frame is timeless."

Cycles Alex Singer

Levallois-Perret, Paris, France

Stepping over the shop threshold of 53 rue Victor Hugo, it is immediately evident that this is a cycling shop steeped in history. The wooden cash register on the counter and the many vintage cycling photos adorning the walls recall a cycling era that people are rediscovering. There is also a range of new and historic bikes on display, including a tandem bicycle on which frame builder Olivier Csuka's mother and father raced. The bike is so well made and immaculately kept that it looks like it was made yesterday. Established by Alex Singer almost 70 years ago, Cycles Alex Singer was successfully operated for 50 years by Ernest Csuka, with the help of his wife, Leone, and his brother, Roland. The family business is still producing finely crafted bicycles and is run by Olivier Csuka, Ernest's son.

Ernest, who died in 2009, having only recently retired from frame-building, served a lengthy apprenticeship alongside Alex and took over the reins a few years before Alex Singer died in 1966. Alex, who was born in Hungary and came to France in 1919, was an excellent randonneur cyclist and the winner of many concours de machines, and in later years was also a competitive racing cyclist. When he ended his cycling

career, Alex decided that he wanted to make his own bicycles. Levallois-Perret in the 1940s was the capital of handmade cars and also supported an aviation industry, so there were many men in the region with exceptional hand and fabricating skills. As there was no recognized bicycle-building industry at the time, the only way to acquire a bicycle was to either make it yourself or approach the growing number of people who could build one for you. In order to make extra money, many men from Levallois-Perret used their skills to construct bicycle frames, and it was in this environment that Alex Singer developed his frame-building skills.

At the time, there were no factory-made bicycle parts so builders had to create their own designs and models and build most parts from scratch. Consequently, much technical innovation occurred as the frame builders were forced to be inventive with their construction and designs. Through sheer ingenuity and resourcefulness, these men hand-produced parts such as derailers, stands, seat posts, cranks, fenders, and all manner of elements used in the production of a functional bicycle. According to Olivier Csuka, Alex Singer was an exceptionally creative man and

worked by himself until Olivier's father Ernest and his uncle became apprentices to him in 1944. Olivier was just a young boy when Alex passed away, but he remembers him as a happy and reserved man and was lucky enough to have spent many hours in the workshop observing and learning the art of fabrication from his father.

Having grown up around bike-building, observing Alex, and learning the art of fabrication from his father, Olivier believes he has a responsibility to carry on the family tradition of bike-building. Although Olivier is involved in other work outside of Cycles Alex Singer, he still continues to build mainly touring bikes in the Alex Singer tradition, while also restoring original Singer bicycles. Olivier is a keen road and track racer and has won a number of championships in more than 30 years of competition. The main priority for Olivier is that his bikes are well crafted and fitted correctly for the bike's purpose. Long-time customer Yannick chose Alex Singer Cycles for its reputation for making the finest bikes. Yannick owns two Singer bikes, a racer, and a randonneur, and recognizes that having a hand-built custom bike made was an investment in cycling for life.

"Having grown up around bike-building, observing Alex Singer, and learning the art of fabrication from his father, Olivier believes he has a responsibility to carry on the family tradition."

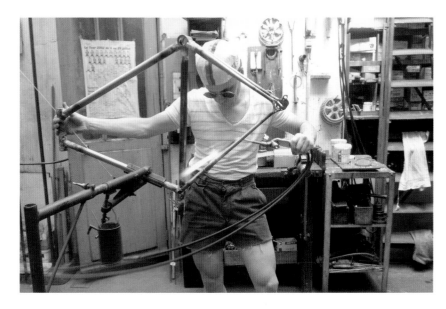

Cyfac

La Fuye, Indre-et-Loire, France

Nestled in France's beautiful Loire Valley, Cyfac has been building custom bicycle framesets since 1982. Home to iconic chateaux, its fair share of world-famous vineyards, and a plethora of picturesque cycling *parcours*, the area's *terroir* and legacy of craftsmanship infuse each Cyfac bike with a distinct character and soul. With Cyfac's unique combination of technological sophistication and artisan quality, each frameset from this passionate company boasts the merits of proper form, fit, and function in one beautiful package.

Cyfac's founder, Francis Quillon, was a former racer and frame-builder. From the outset, his guiding focus was the quest for technological and sporting advancement. He based his designs on craftsmanship and the latest innovations in order to deliver high-quality, cutting-edge products. Today, the craftsmen at Cyfac continue Francis' passion for custom-made frames through the design elements, materials, fabrication techniques, and painting process expressed in their handmade craftsmanship and finish. Cyfac's co-owner and managing director, Aymeric Lebrun, underscores the focus on aesthetics, "We have an *orfèvre* finish, which approaches near perfection with the presence of an invisible weld line

on our aluminum and non-lugged steel frames and flawless tube junctions on our carbon models."

Cyfac builds its bikes from a range of materials and appreciates each for different reasons. Steel is firmly embedded into the beginning of Cyfac's long history and has advantages in terms of comfort and the ability to be repaired anywhere in the world. Cyfac produced some of the first alloy frames in the racing world, as the first manufacturer to master the tungsten inert gas (TIG) method of welding aluminum. Some of the sport's most successful riders, including Laurent Fignon, Marco Pantani, and Richard Virenque, raced on Cyfac alloy creations under the guise of other brands. Alloy is preferred for its reactivity, the quality of the welds, and lightness of the frames. Cyfac built the first alloy frames that were raced in the Tour de France and still values alloy's unique qualities.

When it comes to building with carbon, the Cyfac team feels that it can produce whatever a customer wishes because there are so many possibilities. The frame can be made stiff or flexible, with a carbon or paint finish. Importantly, the carbon frames are light, comfortable, and durable. Cyfac is the only builder in

the world using strategically placed Kevlar layers to improve ride quality and enhance overall durability. It also combines the two "noble" materials of titanium and carbon to build a traditional but very high-tech frame that pairs the natural comfort of titanium with the road filtration and stiffness of carbon.

For Le Brun, managing Cyfac provides a constant sense of excitement because his work varies from day to day and because the range of skills executed by the production team is world-class. "For carbon frames, the wrapping process is most interesting, but for all the frames, the painting process is the most inspiring because it requires precision, patience, and skill." When fitting customers for a new bike, Cyfac has developed its own system, referred to as the Cyfac Postural System. It allows Cyfac to optimize rider comfort, performance, and wellbeing by following stringent, laboratory-proven criteria.

At the end of each day Aymeric likes to look at the wonderful frames his craftsmen have produced, take photos to send to customers who are anxiously awaiting their new Cyfac bicycle, and, weather allowing, ride his own bike home to enjoy the fruits of

Cyfacs look fast just sitting still

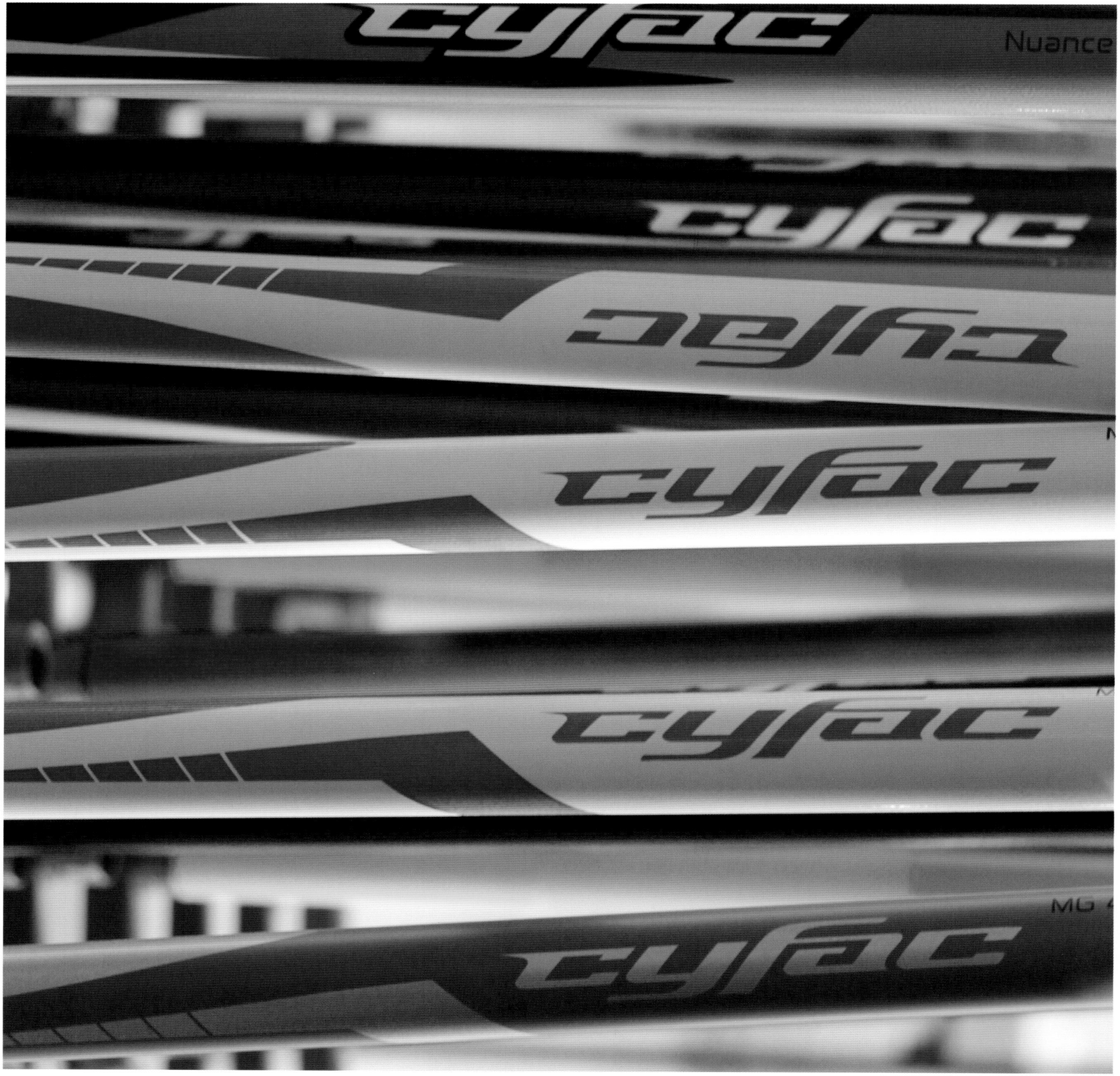
cyfac
Nuance
cyfac
cyfac
cyfac
cyfac
cyfac

"For carbon frames, the wrapping process is the most interesting, but for all the frames, the painting process is the most inspiring because it requires precision, patience, and skill."

Cyfac's custom GOTHICA; 14,000 possible paint tints yield unique custom creations

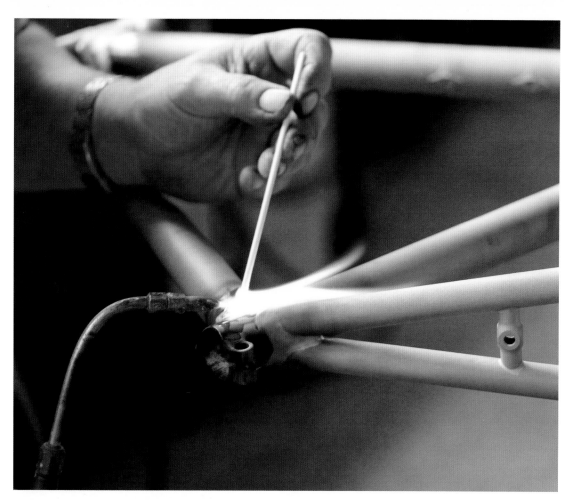

"We have an orfévre finish, which approaches near perfection with the presence of an invisible weld line on our aluminum and non-lugged frames and flawless tube junctions on our carbon models."

Davidson Handbuilt Bicycles

Seattle, Washington, USA

Bill Davidson was a young, impressionable fellow in the early 1970s when the United States was experiencing a bike boom. At the time, Bill was into running but had friends who were into cycling, so decided he would give "this cycling thing" a go. Cycle racing was hugely popular in British Columbia, which was only three hours' ride from Seattle, and Bill would head there with his cycling friends most weekends for some road racing. The European cycling heritage and influence was much stronger in Canada, and Bill admits that he and his friends didn't have much of a clue and were "shredded" every weekend by the better-trained and tactical Canadian riders.

Although cycling was bigger than baseball at the turn of the 20th century in the United States, the advent of the car and improved public transport meant that interest in cycling gradually fell away. Bill's father had established a welding shop in Seattle after World War II that fabricated all sorts of mechanical parts, so Bill spent much of his youth surrounded by machining, welding, and painting.

When he started building bikes, it was a one-man operation, so he was involved in every single step of the process. Bill would measure the customer, design the frame, purchase and install the componentry, paint the frame, fit the customer to the bike, and finally sit back and watch as each proud owner rode off with a new hand-built Davidson bicycle. During that process, there were also several other bikes waiting for Bill to work on, all at different stages of production.

Seven hundred frames later, Bill realized that, "It was going to be a tough row to hoe to do business this way," and decided that he needed to focus his experience and expertise where it was most needed. He realized that his skills would be best served in fitting the customer, helping them arrive at the ideal bike, and specifying the right components, so he employed specialized staff to assist him in his workshop. Davidson bikes are built from beginning to end under the one roof at Bill's workshop in Elliott Bay, Seattle; this way, Bill is able maintain his high production standards and supervise the entire

process. He's also constantly looking for new and interesting ways of producing his bikes, which is why he builds with titanium and carbon fiber in addition to more traditional materials and methods.

As a master builder with almost 40 years of experience behind him, Bill is committed to helping young people who are open-minded, eager, and show aptitude for frame building. Bill mentors this next generation of bike builders at his workshop, where he likes to foster the pride that one gets from executing specific skills in the best possible way. He also has a philosophy of empowering the people that work with him and encourages them to come up with new ideas and innovations for Davidson bikes.

Donhou Bicycles

Norwich, United Kingdom

Tom's background is in product design. He had a job designing toys and perfume bottles for the high street; as much fun as it could be, he was essentially designing disposable consumer goods and it affected his conscience, so he quit and hit the road! He rode his push-bike from Ulan Baataar in Mongolia across the Gobi Desert, down through China, into the Himalayas then down into Vietnam, Laos, Thailand, Malaysia and Singapore: 9000 miles and 9 months. He was on his own so he got a lot of time to think, and while riding he was basically redesigning his expedition bike as he went. That then turned into designing other bikes until he figured out that he wanted to start building frames, one at a time, with as much control over everything as possible.

"On reflection, the more I thought about it, the more I wondered why it took me so long to figure it out. I grew up on bikes. My uncle got me my first BMX and I used it to ride around with friends on the pavement out the front of my house. A few years later he would drop off recumbents he'd been working on in his factory. My dad got me an old Peugeot racer and I thought I was going to win the Tour de France! Then I got into racing mountain bikes, winning the first national downhill I entered. Pretty soon after that I went off to study design and learn how to make things and I worked as a bicycle messenger to pay my way. After time spent on a BMX, a little time on my old Schwinn with my surfboard strapped to my homemade trailer, I now found myself commuting around London on my old messenger bike."

Apart from materials the only thing that gets outsourced is the laser-cutting, and even that is just around the corner. It's important to keep things as close to home as possible. Tom's workshop is small, but just big enough to do what he needs to do. A typical day's work consists of getting up, riding down to the workshop, putting a to-do list together for the day and getting on with what needs doing. Typically there's some emails or admin to sort in the morning, but then Tom can get on with the business of building frames. "The most important thing in building a bike is to be able to communicate its potential. You're going to have amazing times when you ride this bike and that's the underlying reason I do what I do."

Each frame is built in-house by hand, one at a time. From picking, cutting, and shaping the tubes, right the way through to the final coat of paint, it is a full custom-build and experience. Every detail is thought over to make sure you receive a perfect bike in aesthetics, fit, and ride. You can be involved as much or as little in the design and build process as you like—riding is about the experience and at Donhou so is the building. For each build there is a high-quality illustration supplied so you know exactly what your frame and bike will look like when it is finally handed over to you.

Using traditional methods but not afraid to throw in a few modern ones, Tom builds beautiful bicycles. They're built with the foundations of clear thinking and a love for working with the customer and the design process in which your dream bicycle is translated from mind to physical being. Parts are sourced from the UK as much as possible, and it's important to be as gentle on the environment as possible. But in the end, it's being handed your bicycle knowing that it's truly an extension of yourself, excited about the road that lies ahead of it.

"The most important thing in building a bike is to be able to communicate its potential. You're going to have amazing times when you ride this bike and that's the underlying reason I do what I do."

"I entered Tom's workshop to be greeted by my new steed, in a fresh coat of gloss gold, with white accents…Beautiful! After the first pedal revolution I knew that this bike ticked all the boxes that previous bikes had lacked. Nimble, responsive, fast, and comfortable: everything I could ever had hoped for—a bike for life! The whole process was an absolute joy and the finished product was the icing on the cake, all down to Tom's knowledge, skill and eye for detail. It's something I urge every cyclist to do at some point in their life. You wont regret it!"

Gavin Buxton, Manufacturing Engineer, Lotus Cars

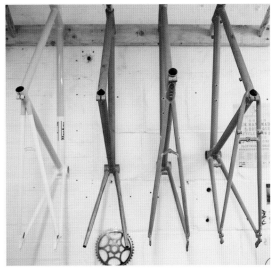

Don Walker Cycles

Louisville, Kentucky, USA

As the founder of the North American Handmade Bike Show, Don Walker has been the driving force behind more than 100 custom bike builders gathering annually to showcase their craftsmanship. Don believes that people are gradually discovering the benefits of owning a custom-made bike because it offers them the opportunity to own a bike that fits them exactly and is an expression of their individuality. He believes that owners of custom-made bikes are saying, "Maybe I don't want to be the guy that keeps showing up for the Saturday morning ride looking like every one else." Don also believes that people are presently rediscovering the joy of getting out in the open air and feeling the rush of wind on their face and through their hair.

Don Walker's passion for cycling was awakened around the age of 14, when everyone in his neighborhood started buying road bikes and going on 25- to 35-mile rides. When he got a bike, he found that his real passion was for track racing and competed in the sport through his high school years. Don loves track racing because of the certain energy that emanates from a velodrome when the riders are battling it out on the track and the spectators

are cheering them on. In his racing days, Don was always ready to do battle on the track and when he discovered around 10 years ago that his surname was connected to a Scottish clan who used to paint their naked bodies blue and run screaming toward their opponents wielding battleaxes and claymores, it went some way to explaining his approach to track cycling. Proud of his Scottish heritage, many of Don's bikes feature tartan paint designs and the decal on each head stem features a tartan background—castle peaks around the shield and two crossed claymores.

Don's bike-building skills were developed over many years while working as an aircraft mechanic. With a passion for track bikes and the skill set to build them, he began producing bikes in California in the 1990s. Since relocating to Louisville, Kentucky in 2011, Don has developed a passion for Cyclo-Cross racing and sponsors a team based there. "Since I've moved to a Cross-centric community, the demand for my cross bikes has gone way up, especially since some of the more prominent locals are racing and winning on them. In the 20 or more years I've been building frames, I had only a few rare orders for cross bikes,

but it seems that they now account for about 20 percent of my overall business."

When a customer comes to Don to be fitted for a bike, he likes to go for a ride with his client to see where they are in relation to the bike. This method means that he can build a more complete picture of the rider's physique and riding style as well as taking the usual measurements. Like so many bike builders who have been building and observing riders for years, Don can usually figure out people's measurements in the first couple of minutes by just looking at them.

Don also likes to include his sense of humor in some of this paint designs. On one of his tandem track bikes, which he refers to as "the tandem of death," the crime scene yellow tape painted on the top tube says: "Crime Scene Do Not Cross." The boom tube that runs between the front and rear bottom bracket features a sidewalk scene with blood and chalk outlines of bodies. "It's a track tandem, they're very dangerous, and not everyone should be riding one. It's like I've got to make it as morbid as I can because if I don't beat somebody on the track, at least I want them to fear me!"

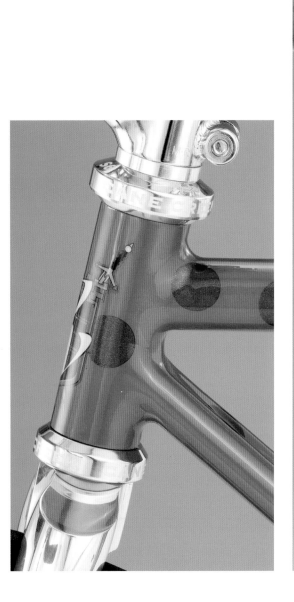

"Maybe I don't want to be the guy that keeps showing up for the Saturday morning ride looking like every one else."

GURU Bicycles

Montreal, Québec, Canada

As an engineering student, cycling fan, and bike aficionado, Tony Giannascoli decided in the mid-1990s to build himself a bike from scratch. He was always taking bikes apart and putting them back together, but couldn't resist adding an extra element in the process. Tony began getting requests from people who admired his bike and from the outset he wanted to custom-build in order to get the perfect fit for optimizing performance. Tony's father is a tailor, so he understands the tradition behind making a bespoke garment for somebody. He quickly found that he was doing things a little differently from the rest of the industry by leaning on his engineering background and finding inspiration from the world of aeronautics to push things forward: "I'm a scientist at heart, so being progressive with materials and methods used is essential for me."

The team of 30 Guru workers produces a range of custom bikes made from carbon, aluminum, titanium, and steel, with each material possessing inherent qualities and characteristics. Tony believes that carbon allows for the creation of the most favorable shapes to deliver optimal stiffness for aerodynamics and ride quality. Building seamless, custom carbon bikes at

Guru is a particular technical challenge and rewarding process. On the other hand, Tony knows there's nothing quite like a beautiful titanium weld and those who ride titanium swear by it.

The Guru team works to the sound of tubes being milled and bikes being buffed as carbon lay-up process specialists, welders, pre-prep, and paint and clear-coating workers go about their daily business. They aim to create a bike that perfectly fits the individual by ensuring that the critical interface between rider and bicycle is set up to achieve optimal power transfer, aerodynamics, and overall ride quality. In terms of the benefits, their customers say that once you have ridden a good custom bike there's no going back. A testament to people's passion for riding a bicycle they love is an 80-year-old Guru customer whose husband follows her every pedal stroke in his car to protect her while she's riding. Jeannine still manages to ride more than 1200 miles every summer.

The attention to detail that goes into customizing a Guru bike is evident in all components, right down to the head badge. The crest containing the logo features a series of dots representing a cross-section of stacked tubes. When one of the tubes is selected for a bike, the right dot on the second row is painted in the same color as the logo, which leaves a capital G in the background. Each head badge is hand-painted to match the client's chosen color scheme, representing Guru's commitment to making bikes one detail at a time. "When you can deliver cutting-edge bikes that are also beautifully handcrafted for one particular person, you're making something special. Honoring those two masters—science and art—is an ongoing challenge for us."

Opposite: Guru Geneo, road bicycle

"I'm a scientist at heart, so being progressive with materials and methods used is essential for me."

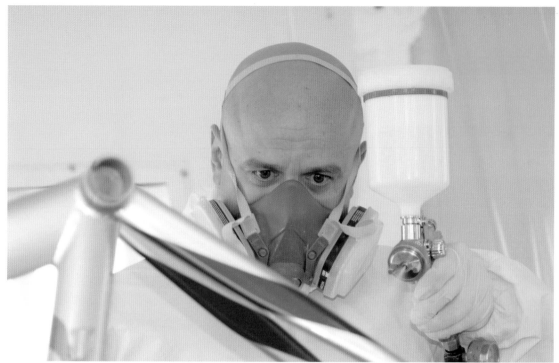

Trained hands and eyes apply a finishing clear coat

The Guru factory, located in Montreal, Canada

Premium-grade carbon fiber is precisely cut based on individual specifications

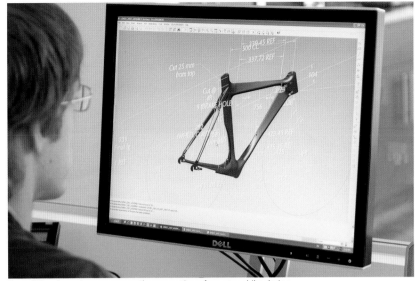
One of Guru's engineers oversees the generation of a custom bike design

Guru's hand-painted head badge (The One) is applied as a crowning jewel

"When you can deliver cutting-edge bikes that are also beautifully handcrafted for one particular person, you're making something special. Honoring those two masters—science and art—is an ongoing challenge for us."

Titanium welded à la Guru

Opposite: Guru Geneo, seamless carbon road frame

The best bike I have ridden …

"When you buy a bike, you think of quite a few different things: the material it's made of, the reputation of the manufacturer, the way it rides, and to be honest, the way it looks. When I bought my Guru Crono from Jack and Adam's in Austin, I spent five hours trying different bikes, different wheel sets, and fiddling with adjustments to get the bikes as close as I could in all ways except the frame. I settled on the Crono because it was, quite simply, the best bike I have ridden in 30 years of riding, including seasons of bike racing and six Ironman Triathlons. It accelerated, it was soft and smooth, it was so responsive. Had someone tried to tell me this in advance, I wouldn't have believed them. But when I rode it, I found myself smiling and shaking my head—truly, I did—on a back road of Austin, because I just didn't know a bike could feel like that."
Peter Stevens

Guru Crono, triathlon / carbon TT Bicycle

Independent Fabrication

Newmarket, New Hampshire, USA

Founded in 1995, Independent Fabrication is a small collective of talented individuals with diverse backgrounds. For some, it is an outlet for creative expression, while for others it is more about the mechanical or technical aspects of fabricating a precision machine. The diversity of backgrounds and overall teamwork of the Independent Fabrication crew give the company great depth, and make the bicycles they produce inherently special. Each member of the team regards bike-building as an honorable profession and an opportunity to work with like-minded individuals who are joined by a common aim of building the best custom bikes that they can.

Independent Fabrication produces a wide range of award-winning bikes, utilizing an equally wide range of materials. Whether working with traditional chromoly steel, modern stainless steel alloys, titanium, or carbon fiber, each Independent Fabrication bike is custom-tailored to meet the unique needs of its owner. Possessing the skills and methods to work across a broad spectrum of models

and materials allows Independent Fabrication to serve customers around the world, both on and off the road, whether racing, commuting, touring, or riding for pleasure.

This flexibility in materials and methods also extends to the bike's aesthetics. Long known for their creative and high-quality paintwork, Independent Fabrication takes great pride in rendering custom finishes. "We believe that a custom bike should not only fit well and ride superbly, but should also reflect the unique personality of its owner. While much ado is justifiably made of the fit and ride quality of a custom bike, our customers are individuals by definition… comfortable in their desire to own a machine that looks as distinctive as it rides. The customised nature of our product and the vast array of material choices, frame options, and aesthetic finishes make our frames and company appealing to all types of bicycle lover."

After more than 15 years of making do in a forlorn industrial space on the wrong side of the railroad tracks, in 2011 Independent Fabrication moved into a beautifully renovated stone mill dating from 1869, alongside the Lamprey River in Newmarket, New Hampshire. This purpose-built space includes a state-of-the-art paint facility, including showroom, fit studio, and employee amenities such as a kitchen, locker room, and a custom bike wash. The new location provides instant access to a vast array of on- and off-road riding, not to mention the phenomenal coffee shop and restaurants just across the street.

When not pursuing their love of cycling through either riding or building bikes, the crew can be found working on vintage motorcycles or houses, building furniture, running, climbing mountains, conquering skate parks, making art, performing music, raising children, and generally enjoying life to the fullest.

Factory signs at the Newmarket Mills

TIG welding a steel frame

"We believe that a custom bike should not only fit well and ride superbly, but should also reflect the unique personality of its owner. While much ado is justifiably made of the fit and ride quality of a custom bike, our customers are individuals by definition…comfortable in their desire to own a machine that looks as distinctive as it rides."

Sanding a fork

Placing decals

Ira Ryan Cycles

Portland, Oregon, USA

One hundred percent pure riding is the passion that carries Ira Ryan to his workshop each day to hand-build his custom bicycles. He has never fitted into one particular category, but describes himself as a cyclist, not a cycling enthusiast. "Anybody on two wheels, as far as I'm concerned, is a friend." He has found working as a bicycle mechanic for the past 15 years, using tools and fixing bikes, a very gratifying experience and considers his hands to be his most important assets.

An adherence to the simplicity of using his hands and minimal tools to create something wonderful is evident in the way Ira works. When designing a bicycle for a customer, there are no computers involved and no complex calculations; however, there is a lot of talking and he likes to draw everything on paper in full size. For the first year and a half of Ira Ryan Cycles, he didn't even have a milling machine, so all the production was done with a hacksaw, files, and sandpaper. Being a bike mechanic and having ridden motorcycles made Ira realize how much specific finessing of design goes into making a custom bicycle. It also made him appreciate the utilitarian nature of bicycles, and the ability to repair them on the side

of the road with a minimal amount of equipment. "Each frame is a step toward an understanding of a craft that takes a lifetime to master and remains difficult to perfect."

When establishing his business it wasn't just the bikes that were paramount—Ira also needed to think about his brand. He made several lists of potential names, but none really stuck, so he settled for Ira Ryan Cycles: "It's your name, it's your bike." At first he found it strange to hear people talk about Ira Ryan as a bike instead of Ira Ryan the person, but having heard it since 2005 he's now used to it. For his head badge, Ira decided to use the image of a swallow. He grew up on a small farm in America's Midwest where the barn swallows would come every summer. The swallow evoked memories of cycle touring and racing in the Midwest—flying down the road on a bike and suddenly riding into a swarm of swallows. It was watching them move and carve the wind that made Ira realize that's what it felt like to ride a bike.

During his time as a bike mechanic, one memory stands out as the first time he experienced the intense feeling of satisfaction from a day's work using your hands and having something to show for it at the end. "It was the face of a child whose training wheels were removed for the first time. It was that feeling of being totally alive, the feeling of freedom, that first exhilarating experience on a bicycle." Ira wants to be part of the next step in bike-building that pushes the boundaries of what is being created today, but is also able to appreciate the beauty of what has been made before. His bicycles are about remembering the roads you have ridden in the past, feeling the experience of those moments, but also looking forward to the many miles of road that you will ride in a lifetime.

"Each frame is a step toward an understanding of a craft that takes a lifetime to master and remains difficult to perfect."

"Anybody on two wheels, as far as I'm concerned, is a friend."

Jeff Jones Custom Bicycles

Medford, Oregon, USA

Jeff Jones has a very straightforward philosophy: "I love riding bikes and the simplicity and joy of the ride, and I strive to build bicycles that best deliver this purity." In his desire to build bikes in which he truly believes, Jeff has bucked the trend of putting suspension on his mountain bikes. He's into performance riding and prefers to do it without suspension. He builds high-performance, non-suspension bicycles built for function, not for fashion, regardless of how it has been done in the past, what the 'latest technology' dictates, and what 'looks' right. Consequently, Jeff is developing bikes with an open mind—using logic, craftsmanship, and hours (and hours) of riding bikes.

He believes that the ride of his bikes is exceptional as the rider isn't isolated from the ground and what's going on beneath them. The rider is riding a bicycle, not a bicycle with a lot of things added to make the trail feel like it's no longer there. You are very much connected to the trail and the bicycle is designed so that you and the bicycle, as one, can immerse yourself in the ride. His bikes ask the rider to pick a line down the trail and to read the terrain. The bike will move with you, responding to the most subtle of

steering gestures and is easy to 'un-weight' up and over obstacles. It doesn't wallow beneath the rider and when you hit the brakes, the bike won't dive. It strips things back to the essence—a pure bicycle—the beautiful simplicity of the frame and forks, the wheels, a saddle and the steering, a crank and the chain.

Jeff is always out on the trails putting his bikes through their paces—customers can see just how capable the bikes are as Jeff rides at a level that most can only aspire to. He has a unique combination of riding ability, creative vision, and practical skills. He finds out exactly what he's going to build when working with a customer on a custom build. He prefers to get out and ride with someone (or watch a video of them cycling if this isn't possible) to watch their riding in order to pick out strengths and weaknesses and see the trails they ride. He asks questions about riding style and the bicycle's intended uses, before handcrafting something truly unique. Jeff has recently developed a range of steel and titanium framesets that he has produced in small batches by hand so that 'the Jones ride' is available to as many people as possible.

Jeff believes in giving a rider space to move around the bike as they ride and a frame that flexes vertically as much as it can—for comfort—while still delivering a horizontal stiffness for efficient pedaling and precise steering. He takes inspiration for the design of his forks from cranes, bridges and early motorcycles, and the frame references the flexible strength of airplane wings. Making the bike work for riding is his only priority and aesthetics take a back seat.

Jeff's workspace is under his house, located up in the woods away from everything. Being there keeps his mind uncluttered and free. He doesn't feel pressure to conform to how anybody else builds mountain bikes. He particularly likes working at night when nobody is around and will sometimes work for 20 hours at a time. He'll just keep going, crashing out when he's done: "It's about the flow, how things are going—you stay in there, you don't have to think about it too much, it just works"—much like his bikes.

Truss fork detail

Why do I love my bike?

"It might be the design and craftsmanship—the unique combination of insight and engineering. It could be the obvious attention to every single detail. I must say I don't love it for its looks—when form follows function you don't get conventional beauty. No, I love my bike because it makes me happy, it makes me smile. There's not been one ride in the years I've had it when it hasn't inspired me and impressed me with its capabilities and appropriateness. There hasn't been one ride when I haven't had my spirits lifted. I'm not one for angles or tubing profiles but I love riding a bike that feels and reacts like it is a part of me."

Anonymous

"Jeff is developing bikes with an open mind—using logic, craftsmanship, and hours (and hours) of riding bikes."

Keith Anderson Cycles

Grants Pass, Oregon, USA

As a child, bicycles gave Keith his first taste of freedom and he's been in love with them ever since. When he was a young man he had worked in a bike shop and was never particularly impressed by the workmanship on even the most expensive bikes. His passion for building bikes came from an overwhelming urge to create something with his own hands and he knew he could create something much better than the mass-produced models that he had seen in his youth.

With every bike he builds, Keith tries to incorporate some type of unique design element and aims never to build the same bike twice. He always looks for ways to personalize a bike for a customer and is very focused on detail, not only for aesthetics but also for functionality. All of Keith Anderson's bikes are built exclusively with steel because he believes that it has a history unmatched by any other material used by man. It has all the properties necessary to make the perfect bicycle—strength, durability, resilience, is easily repairable, readily available, relatively cheap, and compared with titanium, aluminum, and carbon fiber, less toxic to produce. "Once put into its final form, steel has a ride that cannot be duplicated."

As somebody with a highly developed artistic flair, Keith feels blessed that he's always had a diverse skill set that has led to him being a bike-builder and painter. He is not only highly regarded as a frame-builder but also as a master painter of bicycle frames, and much of his time is spent doing paintwork for other builders. Although he loves every aspect of the bike-building process, Keith says, "The transformation that takes place during the painting process is like a butterfly emerging from its chrysalis. It has metamorphosed from something dark and monochromatic into something rich and colorful."

Like any business, there are other aspects to be taken care of and Keith's assistant Corey helps him to keep focused on production. Corey takes care of the digital artwork creation, website development, answering phones, shipping, and whatever else it takes to run a contemporary bike-building business. Music is also a constant in Keith and Corey's working day and is played through a CD changer, a decent-sized amp, and four booming speakers. The workspace also includes a couple of guitars and a drum set ready for those times when inspiration strikes and also for Keith and Corey to have a jam session at the end

of the day. They always have fun at work, which Keith believes is an important ingredient in maintaining a good working environment. Apart from the Keith Anderson head badge, affectionately know as "Howdy Sprocket," Keith's favorite feature on a bike is the rider: "Without the rider it's just a piece of functional art … bicycles are just like guitars, they are tools to be used, no matter how beautiful."

*"Without the rider it's just a piece of functional art …
bicycles are just like guitars, they are tools to be used,
no matter how beautiful."*

Keith Anderson logo in 24k gold leaf

"*The transformation that takes place during the painting process is like a butterfly emerging from its chrysalis. It has metamorphosed from something dark and monochromatic into something rich and colorful.*"

Etched sterling-silver head badge

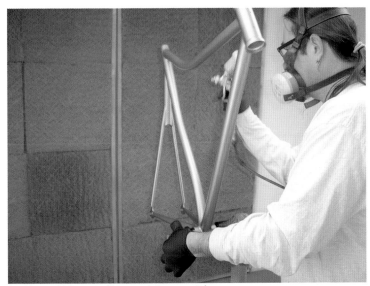

Applying multiple coats of blue candy to a pursuit frame

Seat cluster showing seat stay top before cap

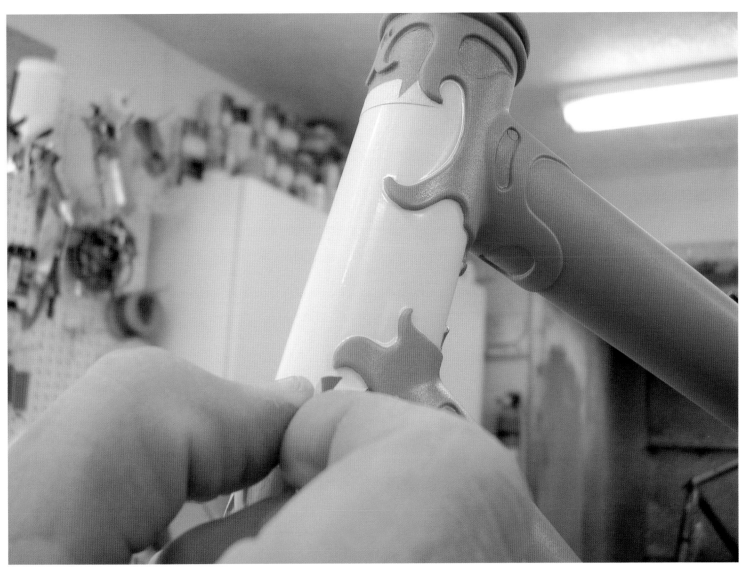

Unmasking the head tube on a Rivendell

Kirk Frameworks

Bozeman, Montana, USA

David Kirk was too young to have one of the racing cars his father built so he had the next best thing, a British Racing Green bicycle with his name emblazoned across the chain guard in chrome lettering. David's father was a racing car mechanic and when it came time for David to get his first bicycle he made one from parts he collected and refurbished, with some new parts thrown into the mix. David had a unique, custom-made bike that opened up his world and allowed him to explore things on his own for the first time. His father instilled in him from day one the concept that bicycles were something one made and not something one bought.

Many years passed between that first bicycle and David becoming a frame builder, but he always knew it would happen, as if he was born to it. Like the cars his father worked on, David's bikes are designed to perform. He likes to think of them as simple and elegant with a look that draws you in for a closer inspection, as opposed to something that shouts at

you. As David explains: "They are sparse and to the point. My favorite car is a Lotus Seven and I would be pleased to have my bikes compared to one." All of David's bikes are built from steel and are either lugged and silver-brazed or fillet-brazed with brass. He loves the way steel rides and the feeling it gives on the road, and having worked with many other materials he prefers it because nothing compares to the way it feels in his hands and the sound it makes when working with it.

As a lone builder, David is involved in all aspects of building, right down to shipping the bikes to their new owners. All Kirk bikes are produced in his garage at home, which has everything he needs plus the added bonus of incredible mountain views. When David constructs his frames he does it in two phases: first the front triangle is built and machined straight and clean; then the rear triangle is added to the front. He believes that working on the front triangle before the rear is added is much easier and more efficient. Adding the rear triangle to the front allows

a view of the entire bike in his mind's eye and enables him to visualize it under the rider on the road, doing what it's meant to do. "Adding the rear is my favorite part because it turns the work from a bunch of tubes to a frame. Even after all these years and thousands of frames I still get excited every time I add the rear triangle."

David's favorite part on a bike is the seat cluster, because there are four tubes coming together as well as the seat post clamp. He likes putting a lot of detail into this area to make it a visual focal point. As a homage to his father, David's DK logo was inspired by the way his father used to mark his own specialized automotive tools with a JK where the back of the J and K were shared. He has also continued his father's love of racing cars by fabricating his own parts and entering autocross events. At the end of the day, David takes time out to look over his work, then watches the orange light of the sunset shining on the Bridger Mountains right in front of his home.

"Adding the rear is my favorite part because it turns the work from a bunch of tubes to a frame. Even after all these years and thousands of frames I still get excited every time I add the rear triangle."

JK Special Classic made for the NAHBS event

Hand lug lining by John Bell

Self portrait in shop

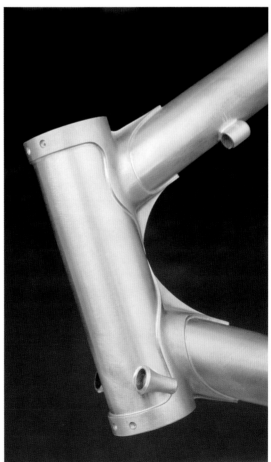

Webbed lugs in the raw

Playing with fire

Unpainted fillet brazed bottom bracket

"My favorite car is a Lotus Seven and I would be pleased to have my bikes compared to one."

Still looks wet

The downhill ride was a thrill …

"I finally got to take my bike up and down a twisting mountain road today, and I can tell you without a doubt, this is the best handling bike I have ever had the privilege of riding. This bike climbed effortlessly without a lot of input on my part. I didn't have to fight to keep my line, though it was responsive when asked to be. The downhill ride was a thrill. I didn't think it was possible, but the bike felt so stable and nimble at the same time. From the very first turn it was silky smooth, though not in the least sluggish. I could drive into a curve and, if need be, change my line at the last minute to maneuver around rocks or sand without any hesitation or protest from the bike. It entered and exited the turns exactly as I wanted and made me wish the ride was longer, something that I haven't experienced in a long time. Dave, I don't know how you did it, but you have the magic touch; I wouldn't change a thing."

Anonymous

Karin Kirk high in the Bridger Mountains

JKS X with Di2 made for NAHBS 2012

JK Special Classic in custom blue

JKS X lower head lug and Di2 port

Kish Fabrication

Carrboro, North Carolina, USA

Performing major surgery on broken bicycles to get to the next destination played a significant part in Jim Kish becoming a bicycle-frame builder. After several years of living out of panniers as a professional bicycle tour leader, Jim needed a new path to follow. One of his favorite parts of touring was the challenge of fixing bikes, so it seemed to be an easy choice to embark on creating his own bike-building business in 1992.

Kish bikes are designed to be as efficient and as simple as possible; nothing is there that doesn't belong. Even the head badge on his bikes is a small, simple K with no interesting story behind it other than it's K for Kish. Jim builds his bikes from titanium and steel, but prefers titanium because he feels that it exhibits the perfect combination: it's strong, lightweight, corrosion-resistant, and provides a smooth ride. In its unpainted state, titanium also has an elegant, yet utilitarian look.

Jim's frame-building philosophy is also reflected in his workspace, which is relatively compact, stocked with very fine tools and fixtures, and kept very clean. If you were to wander into Jim's workspace today, you may hear some psychedelic rock, ambient, bluegrass, or metal music wafting from the stereo system, as music provides a constant backdrop to his working day. His dog is also there to keep him company as she sleeps away the day on her bed. Jim's workshop space, tools, and equipment also come in handy for both family and friends when something needs fixing or to build car parts, furniture, or any other widget that may be needed.

The problem-solving process of the fitting and frame design are Jim's favorite part of bike-building. When taking a customer's body and current bike measurements, he also weighs up their athletic experience and riding style. Jim believes that while most people could fit comfortably on a stock bicycle, everyone can benefit in some way by owning a custom-built bike. It may simply be a detail in the fit, the tubing selection to complement riding style, or the fittings to match individual needs or aesthetic preference that make it all worthwhile. Jim has particularly enjoyed working with customers who have been architects, photographers, and musicians because they have all shared a similar sense of a bicycle's purpose and a "less is more" aesthetic.

Jim is kept very busy these days building bikes for other people to ride. He no longer has the time to go on long bike tours, but he does use his bike to run errands and tries to get out on a long mountain or road ride at least once a week. Jim's philosophy in a nutshell: "The ultimate feature of a bike is its intangible capability to motivate one to ride more and get healthier."

Town bike with rack

TI road bike with back end

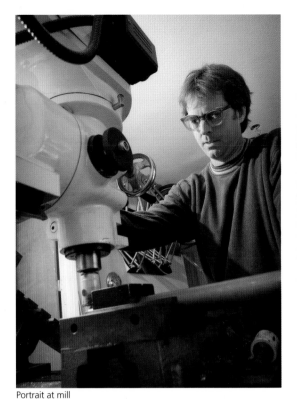
Portrait at mill

Welding

"The ultimate feature of a bike is its intangible capability to motivate one to ride more and get healthier."

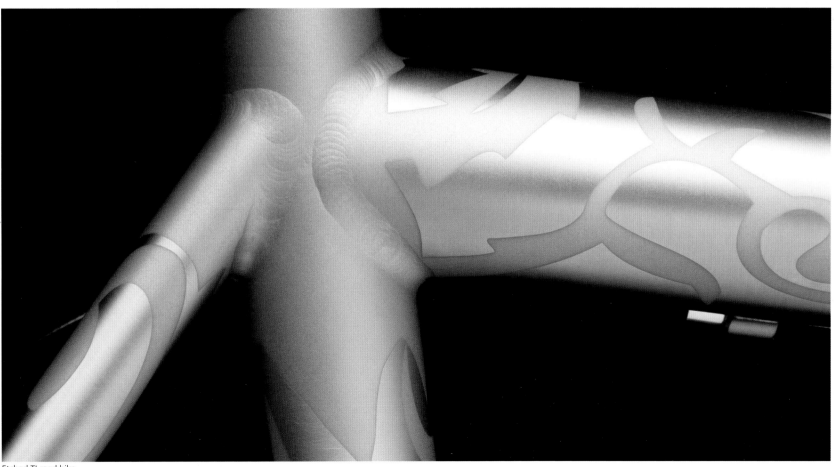
Etched TI road bike

Painted TI 29er

Mountain bike bottom bracket

Jim's process is clear and enlightening …

"After researching many titanium frame builders, I finally decided to meet with Jim Kish first and I never contacted any other builder. From the outset, his courtesy, experience, attention to detail, enthusiasm, and professionalism were clearly evident. I immediately ordered a custom titanium and I have been completely satisfied ever since. Jim's process is clear and enlightening, the fit is perfect, the craftsmanship is excellent, the finish is gorgeous, and the ride is superb."

Tomaso Bradshaw, Venice, California

650 B MTN bike

Llewellyn Custom Bicycles

Everton Hills, Queensland, Australia

From an early age, Darrell McCulloch played intensely with his Lego. This creative focus was a precursor to building model railways and Airfix plane kits as he grew older. At school he was naturally drawn to art, woodwork, metalwork, and technical drawing, and at home he was always tinkering with bikes. Fitness has been an important part of Darrell's life from a young age; his family didn't own a car so bikes were a natural choice of transport. Two *Bicycling* magazine articles describing custom bicycle frame building and a story about a team mechanic further sparked Darrell's passion for bikes and cycling. At this point in time he was a keen athletics competitor, but decided to switch from athletics to cycle racing as his interests in all things cycling grew stronger.

After leaving school, Darrell got a job with one of the few frame builders in Queensland and worked with him for six-and-a-half years and later in other bike shops. Darrell had a vision of where he wanted to be and established Llewellyn Custom Bicycles toward the end of 1988 as a part-time affair. During this period he was also racing bikes in France, working with cycling teams as a mechanic, and coming home for the summer. He counts himself very fortunate that he had the experience of traveling to 21 different countries with the Australian Institute of Sport as their road-cycling mechanic and an equipment supplier for the men's and women's road teams. In 2001, Darrell chose to devote his full energies to Llewellyn Custom Bicycles because he knew that building bespoke bicycles was how he wanted to express himself.

Over the years, Darrell has developed and pursued his own style and techniques for creating beautifully crafted lugged-steel bicycles. His grandfather's words, "Don't rest till your best is better," are a constant inspiration to Darrell and each week he sets out to better what he did the week before at the workbench. "Many details and techniques would make not one difference to the client's perception of their Llewellyn cycle, but are done for my satisfaction. For me to know that a particular detail or step is inserted sates my pursuit of purity in the frame-construction process."

Darrell uses high-quality butted-steel tubing and lugged construction for its superb ride qualities and proven durability. This method offers endless possibilities and flexibility for his expression of design and aesthetics, including intricate detailing if desired. Many parts and features on a Llewellyn bike are made from stainless steel because he feels this material also has merit. Aesthetics are important to Darrell, but durability and function will never be sacrificed. "My desire is to create a bicycle for my client that gives them many years of enjoyable riding, so with each passing year the bicycle gives them more value. Thus they come to cherish their Llewellyn."

Darrell works alone at the bench, manipulating the tubes and lugs, wielding the brazing torch, and guiding the files with his hands. His painter Joe Cosgrove gives each Llewellyn bike its beautiful paint finish, allowing Darrell to be intensely absorbed with the design and form of the metalwork. In keeping with his lifetime of fitness, Darrell gets out to ride most days for two or three hours in the surrounding hills and mountains, with a longer ride with his mates on Sundays. Bikes have given Darrell many great travels and friends from around the world and he is grateful that his passion is constantly enhanced by the enjoyment he gets from clients using his bicycles.

Finish work on a lugged stem

Nine hours were spent on this custom handmade lug

Stainless steel details

At the alignment table

"Many details and techniques would make not one difference to the client's perception of their Llewellyn cycle, but are done for my satisfaction. For me to know that a particular detail or step is inserted is to sate my pursuit of purity in the frame-construction process."

It feels like nothing I've ever ridden...

"By way of touring bike—completely assured, responsive, poised, and gorgeous to look at. A friend described it as an interesting mix of retro looks (the frame geometry, quill, cantilever brakes, and color scheme) coupled with modern components. I think he's right. At first glance it looks like a well-preserved 35-year-old bike, but on closer examination you realize that all the components are current. It leans beautifully into corners, the cantilever brakes pull it up much better than side-pulls ever could, it absorbs road shocks exceptionally well and exceptionally quietly, and it doesn't complain about anything throw at it but seems to keep saying "bring it on—is that all you've got?"
Christopher L.

Details cut into stainless steel dropouts

Hand-cut and polished stainless lugs

Hand-cut stainless details

No chrome! Llewellyn with stainless lugs.

Lynskey Performance Designs

Chattanooga, Tennessee, USA

Lynskey Performance Designs is very a much a family-operated company with a burning desire to produce high-quality, custom-made performance bikes that are also functional pieces of art. Mark Lynskey and his siblings grew up around the tools and machinery of their father's Chattanooga machine shop, which was established in the 1960s when Chattanooga was one of the largest industrial centers in the United States. Mark is a mechanical engineer by profession and specialized in exotic metals fabrication. It was through one of Mark's younger brothers that the family turned their experience and expertise of metal fabrication into making bikes.

David Lynskey took up cycling when he had to give up running because of a knee injury. When it came to getting a bike for himself, it was a natural progression to look no further than his family's machining business. By the late 1980s, after David had made other bikes for friends, it was clear to the family that David's bike-building was a path that they wanted to pursue and they were interested in producing their own brand of bicycles. The idea proved to be highly successful, and by the mid-1990s it was all that the business was producing. Over that time, they built a

reputation as a world leader in high-performance titanium bikes and the firm was eventually acquired by another company.

After a period of time, the Lynskey family decided that they wanted to do something together, and through their mother Ruby's encouragement it was decided that they would again start building bicycles because of their love of working with metal and their desire to be involved with an active sport. The family enjoys working with elite athletes through to recreational riders and loves the challenge of building bikes that are not just individually tailored, but also high performance and suited to owners' particular needs. The real spirit and goal of what they are constantly trying to achieve is: "To have a bike that does exactly what you want it to do, fits you exactly the way you want it to fit, and looks exactly as your heart desires."

All five members of the Lynskey family have designated roles in the business and have complementary skills for producing their range of custom bikes. Mark's primary roles are bike design, sales, and marketing; the next eldest brother, David, is also involved with the bike designs and oversees the running of the workshop as

well as designing tools and equipment. The second-youngest brother is Chris, who does all the engineering drawings, his wife Toni is the welder, and the youngest brother Tim runs the finishing department and final inspection. Finally, Ruby and her daughter Theresa play active roles in the business on a daily basis by running the accounts department. Although Mark Lynskey's father passed away a number of years ago, he is still very much a part of the Lynskey brand with his signature appearing on the head badge. Also featured on the badge is a shamrock, to reflect Lynskey's Irish heritage, and a tethered hunting hawk from the Thompson family crest, which refers to their mother's maiden name and British heritage.

The Lynskey Backroad is designed specifically for trans-continental, fully-loaded touring. It is also available with S&S Couplers.

A custom 29er built for Ed Ibbetson, Manager of Lynskey's UK distributor, Hotlines

The Lynskey R230 with S&S Couplers and one of Lynskey's classic houseblend panels paint schemes

The Lynskey Pro29 VF with a custom flames paint job

"To have a bike that does exactly what you want it to do, fits you exactly the way you want it to fit, and looks exactly as your heart desires."

The Lynskey R340 with custom geometry and beautiful cobalt blue paint

Marschall Framework

Moehnesee, Germany

Uwe Marschall's passion for bikes was ignited at the age of 13, when he visited a bike workshop. As he grew older, he began competing in bike races with much success. As a lone frame builder, Uwe has been constructing tailor-made road racing, touring, and mountain bikes since 1991, and also makes tandems and bikes for children. The inspiration for his designs is taken from the classic Italian designs, noted for their clean lines and aesthetic appeal.

His choice of frame-building material is steel and stainless steel, which he prefers for their strength and versatility. The frames can be finished in a shining wet lacquer or a natural non-lacquered look that can be brushed finished or highly polished, using high-grade steel. For those customers who wish to add

color to their frame, there are a number of specialized paintwork designs and colors from which to choose. Uwe also likes to build with steel because, from an environmental point of view, he believes it is far more eco-friendly than other materials, due to lower energy consumption in the extraction process.

Building a bike that fits a customer exactly is paramount to Uwe, and he therefore conducts an exhaustive measuring process and detailed discussion about personal preferences and the purpose for which the bike will be ridden. All of these elements are taken into consideration before Uwe enters the data into a specialized computer program that he

uses to calculate and determine the correct geometry for the bike frame. One of the most important features to be placed on his bikes is the Marschall Framework star. The head badge is the final piece to be placed on any individual bike before it is handed over to the customer. For Uwe, it marks the end of his building process and the beginning of a wonderful riding experience for the new owner.

Moots

Steamboat Springs, Colorado, USA

Moots is located high in the mountains in a small ski resort town called Steamboat Springs. It's a very remote area and sits at about 7,000 feet of elevation on the west side of the Rockies. The 25 full-time employees work in a modern, clean facility and are very much a part of the town community; they help the locals maintain a piece of forested property that has world-class trails located just above the town. During the summer months, mountain bike riders have access to miles of pristine, tall-wooded areas in which to enjoy the fresh mountain air while riding their bikes along sun-filtered trails.

As a company, Moots aims to be environmentally responsible by keeping cars out of their parking lot as much as possible. They encourage their employees to ride to work and have a company commute policy where employees earn credits towards bike parts. It's all part of a broader Moots philosophy to build beautiful bikes with a ride quality that will find you choosing to ride to work or run errands on your bike rather than taking the car.

Their regard for the environment also permeates through the workplace, where they recycle everything they use, including all metals and cardboard, instead of sending it to landfill. The company has recently installed a system of large solar panels to help offset the energy used in making their bikes. The Moots staff come from a wide variety of backgrounds and whether they have worked in bike shops, studied bike-building at frame school, toured the world on a bike, or raced professionally, they all have something in common— a passion for bikes and cycling.

When Moots started building bikes in 1981, they built nothing but steel custom road bikes, which evolved into their first steel mountain bike. In 1990, Moots switched to making bikes from titanium and have since been thoroughly dedicated to building all their bikes from this material. As a metal, titanium not only suits the Moots philosophy of building a product that is long-lasting, but it also works well with their bike designs.

It's important to Moots that their customers have an enjoyable experience right from the beginning because most often they have saved and saved for the bike of their dreams, and when people are spending that sort of money it's important that everything is done correctly. The Moots custom-fitting process is facilitated through their vast, worldwide network of dealers and they seek out only high-quality suppliers who are experienced and efficient in the fitting process.

As a testament to handmade custom bicycles being bikes for a lifetime, customers will often send bikes that they've owned for many years back to the Moots factory to be reblasted and decaled. The holistic approach that Moots has developed over the years towards its employees, their community, the environment, their bike-building, and ultimately their customers, is a model to be proud of. The Moots philosophy is reflected in the clean lines of their bike designs and the idea that a well-made bike crafted by highly skilled people can become an heirloom that is passed down through generations for many years to come.

Naked Bicycles and Design

Quadra Island, British Columbia, Canada

Naked Bicycles and Design, run by Sam Whittingham and his wife Andrea, is located on Quadra Island, four hours' drive north of Victoria, British Columbia, and is accessible by a small ferry from Vancouver Island. The workshop's remote location means that many Naked bikes are built by long-distance correspondence with the client, so detailed conversations over the telephone or email are extremely important to the fitting and design process. However, when Sam meets customers face-to-face he relishes the opportunity to perform a personalized fitting. As part of this fitting process, Sam likes to head out for a ride with his customers so that he can fully analyze each client's riding style, skill level, and ride preferences. In order for Sam to custom-build the right bike, it is vital that he understands both the personality and cycling needs of his customers.

Sam's driving passion to build bikes was nurtured by doing a lot of bike touring with his dad. He has also raced both mountain and track bikes and was on the Canadian National Track Team for a number of years; remarkably, one of his claims to fame is his inclusion in the *Guinness Book of Records* for a speed bike

record. Before he embarked on setting up his own bike-building business, Sam worked for many years as a bike-fitter and spent a lot of time measuring customers and working off their current bikes. This experience helped shape his bike-building philosophy: "Fitting the man to the machine, that's my thing. Making them one with the bike, which you can only do with custom."

The name Naked reflects one of Sam's core attitudes: "My desire is to build bikes unadulterated by hype and the latest fads." For Sam, it is crucial that his custom bikes not only fit each customer perfectly, but are also reliable and built to last: "I know I can build a steel bike that in 20 years is not going to crack." Although Sam is mostly called upon to build basic, everyday TIG-welded bikes, he is able to indulge in more intricate design features when a customer requests a lugged bike. With a background in theatrical costume and set design, Sam's creative skills really come to the fore when he wants to build a special bike. For the 2007 North American Handmade Bike Show, Sam combined all of his bike-building skills and creative flair to build an exceptional show bike. Features such as wooden

wheel rims, the extensive use of chrome, and angled sculptured handlebars with wooden grips caught the eye of a Tour de France winner, who subsequently acquired the award-winning bike for his collection.

Sam's passion for building bikes is often reflected back to him from his equally passionate customers. He has one such client who regularly keeps Sam updated with the life and times of his bike by sending him pictures of his cycling adventures. Whether Sam's breaking speed records or designing eye-catching show bikes, you can be sure that Naked is about form, function, and line.

The bike rocks ...

"It climbs fast, isn't twitchy on the downhill, and it rails turns.
The bike rocks, you did a great job!"

Mike Morgan, California

All paint is done in the Naked workshop

Naked fabricates many of its own parts

All Naked bikes are built with love and logic

Custom spoke shave handlebars

"My desire is to build bikes unadulterated by hype and the latest fads."

Naked detailing, including e-centric dropouts

Pegoretti

Trento, Italy

Dario Pegoretti's journey into bike-building began out of necessity—his father-in-law required some help in his workshop and Dario needed some cash. Although he admits the passion grew slowly, once it was ignited he developed a true hunger to start building his own frames. After learning his craft from Gino Milani in the great Italian frame-building tradition, Dario was keen to apply his own ideas to frame-building.

Over the years, Dario built up a reputation in the professional riding scene, and found himself building frames for elite riders and teams in Europe thanks to the particular ride characteristics of his bikes. Dario also raced as a young man, but doesn't get out to ride as much as he would like these days because he is so busy creating bikes for customers. Dario's workshop is located in Caldonazzo, a beautiful resort town in the Dolomites, just a few minutes' ride from his home, near Trento.

Dario builds a range of bikes from steel and aluminum, but has a preference for steel because it allows for the most control in the building process and provides the best ride qualities. Pegoretti bikes also have a reputation for their unique paint schemes, optional designs, colors, and finishes, which transform the bike into a rolling piece of art. When somebody owns a custom Pegoretti bike, they not only have a bike that suits their body and riding requirements, but will also be riding on top of more than 25 years of experience from a master builder who has put his own stamp on bike design and built bikes for some of the top riders in the world.

It is very important to Dario for people to understand that his bikes are handmade, and this is evident in his head badge. The Pegoretti head badge, which is fixed to the frame with machine screws, is made of steel with a stylized "P" and a hand to signify that the frame is *fatti con le mani:* "made with hands." Assisted by Pietro and Daniel in his workshop, many a Pegoretti bike has been born to the sounds of blues and jazz floating through the workshop from the horn speakers and valve amplifier.

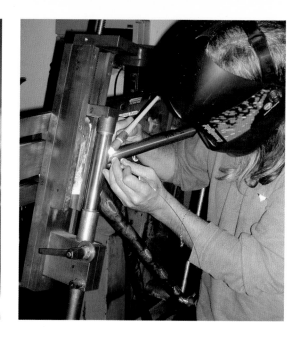

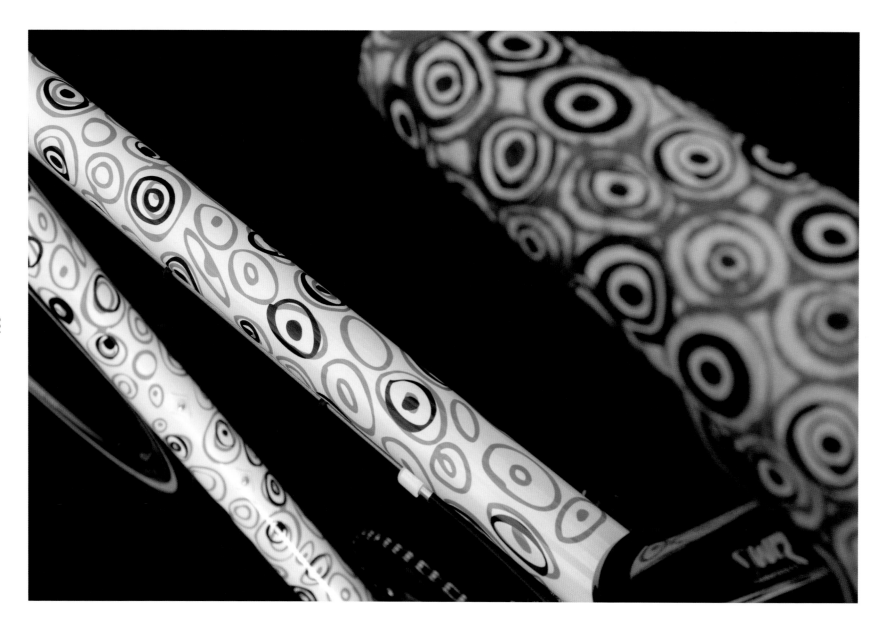

Richard Sachs Cycles

Warwick, Massachusetts, USA

A self-confessed rebel, Richard Sachs describes his passion and addiction to bikes and racing as continually evolving and believes that he came to build bikes serendipitously. At the age of 16, he was smitten with his 10-speed bike and eventually started subscribing to biking magazines and learning about bike racing. What he does as a bike-builder is inseparable from the sport of racing, something that became embedded in his psyche back in the 1960s: "The needle kind of got in my arm once I learned the connection between bicycles and the sport of bike racing." On completing high school he couldn't get into college in September and had to wait until April. With time to kill, he wrote to several bike-builders in England, hoping that he'd be able to travel and learn how to make bikes. Fortunately, one person offered him such an opportunity, and he headed off to England for a year and worked as an apprentice at Witcomb Cycles.

Richard is also a confirmed loner and over the years has never felt the need to take on an apprentice himself, for a number of reasons. He and many of his contemporaries learned their craft hands-on in the bicycle-production arena and he believes that without doing tasks repetitively and without seeing things done time after time, hour after hour, you can't possibly glean enough from a frame-builder to become a frame-builder. As a master frame-builder himself with some 40 years' experience, Richard believes that the learning never ends and that you never fully understand what you're doing. As he says, "You can believe you've mastered it or attained it, but before you know it something will happen and after all those years you've been doing it a certain way, you just realize that you can do it better or more efficiently."

Recent years have seen an increasing preoccupation with the importance of frame materials relative to a bicycle's performance. For some companies, only tubing recently declassified by the Department of Defense will do. Some claim that their bicycles are designed by "real engineers with real degrees", while others entice you with leaflets depicting bar graphs and CAD/CAM jargon to legitimize their products. In contrast to all this, Richard does things the "old" way and claims that few bicycle-makers can offer the rider a frame built as well as his.

Richard not only tries to perfect his own skills on a daily basis, but is also passionate about passing on his knowledge and experience to others in his own way. As a prolific blogger, he spends a lot of time on message boards answering questions and providing links to his Flickr pages. There is also the Richard Sachs cyclocross team, in which Richard regularly competes with just as much conviction as in his younger days. He has been told on numerous occasions that: "He's got it licked." He works for himself, he likes what he does, he's in demand, and he describes the town where he lives as like heaven on earth.

Richard and his wife recently moved to a mountaintop hamlet with just 710 inhabitants, on a six-acre plot with no neighbors in sight. He is totally focused when building and likes to work in silence, as to him, any sound is a distraction that takes him away from being at one with the art of frame-building. The type of customer who wants a Richard Sachs lugged-steel racing bike comes to him with an understanding of his emotions, his thoughts, and his racing team, and after being in the business for a long time, Richard feels blessed that the kind of orders he gets suits the type of bikes that he wants to make.

"The needle kind of got in my arm once I learned the connection between bicycles and the sport of bike racing."

"You can believe you've mastered it or attained it, but before you know it something will happen and after all those years you've been doing it a certain way, you just realised you can do it better or more efficiently."

Roark Custom Titanium Bicycles

Brownsburg, Indiana, USA

Roark is an aerospace company that has been producing jet engine parts for almost 60 years. Within the same facility, a group of three employees also makes beautifully crafted titanium bikes. This connection between bicycles and flying has a famous precedent—the Wright brothers drew inspiration for developing their flying machines from bicycles. According to Jim Zoellner, one of the bike-building team, Roark, as opposed to the Wright brothers, took their inspiration from the aerospace industry and applied their specific knowledge of aviation to the design and production of titanium bicycles.

Roark builds a range of custom bikes that are designed to suit each individual rider perfectly. There are two local fitters in Indianapolis and authorized fitters all over the world; these technicians fit each customer on an adjustable-fit bike and spend two to three hours with them making the necessary adjustments and discussing the fit and measurements. Once the session is complete, this information is sent to the bike-building team at Roark and the frame is designed accordingly. With access to the best materials and equipment, highly skilled industrial designers, and metalworkers, Roark is able to build high-quality

custom bikes for people with a great passion for cycling, whether they are casual riders or hardcore racers. Over the past 10 years or so, the company has also sponsored one of the top amateur cycling teams in the United States, the Texas Roadhouse Cycling Team. The team has been very successful and has won approximately 20 national championships riding Roark racing bikes.

The bike-building team at Roark are not only adept at building a wide range of bikes, but when a special bike order is required they are limited only by their imagination in utilizing the high-tech equipment and incorporating aerospace materials into the design. Jim Zoellner wanted to make a special bike for his young daughter and came up with the idea of laser-cut butterfly wheel spokes, which is only one of the many distinguishing artistic features on this bicycle. The head badge and butterflies dotted all over the bike's frame were made from a stainless steel mesh designed for use on a nuclear submarine. With its curved tubing frame design, custom chain guard,

and personally engraved seat, it is the type of bike that can go on to become a family heirloom: "The bike is a beautiful thing. You think back to some of your best childhood memories and many of them contain bicycles."

Roark track bike—2007 NAHBS Best Titanium Bike

"The bike is a beautiful thing. You think back to some of your best childhood memories and many of them contain bicycles."

Titanium chain guard

SRAM I-Motion 9-speed hub resides inside custom billet 16-inch wheel

Roark show bike for 2008 NAHBS

Robin Mather

Bristol, United Kingdom

Robin Mather has been building lugged and fillet-brazed steel frames in the south west of England for the past 20 years. The passion that drives him more than anything else is the creative process in the workshop and being able to lose himself in imagining, designing, and finally realizing a small detail. Robin has always been interested in how things are constructed and grew up in a woodworking environment where tools, equipment, and workshop space were always available. He believes that there is something intrinsically wonderful about cycling and is not driven by the belief that there is only one way to build a bicycle.

Robin started building frames with steel because of its relative affordability and accessibility. He still feels that as a material, it offers plenty of opportunities and challenges. Although he is also interested in the possibilities of other materials, he is content to leave them for other bike-builders to explore. Each frame he makes is individually considered and is the end result of the customer's needs and preferences. Robin Mather likes to innovate, but is well aware of the 100 years of evolution that the bicycle has undergone.

He derives satisfaction from executing conventional design well and ensuring that every detail of the bike is finished as well as it can be. In his own way, he also likes to advocate the use of bikes for transport and particularly enjoys making functional, versatile bikes.

Robin's approach to bike-fitting is flexible, as he builds a wide range of bike types, from expedition tourers to fast randonneur and single-speed 29ers, and doesn't believe that there is one fit system that can cope with every situation. He places great emphasis on a customer's existing bike and their subjective experience, as well as considering the intended function, level of fitness, flexibility, and aspirations of each customer. Where possible, he also likes to go for a short ride with his clients to observe their riding style.

Robin has recently moved to a new workshop in the centre of Bristol and enjoys exploring the city and the surrounding countryside on two wheels. Occasionally, he will head off-road as he loves to tour. As well as numerous tours in France, he has taken trips in Italy, Iceland, Norway, and even Ethiopia.

Like many frame-builders, Robin Mather's business has grown organically out of a hobby, by first building bikes for himself, then for friends who have become customers. He is now fortunate that many of his customers have become friends.

Reynolds 725 tubes silver-brazed into a modified Pacenti bottom head lug

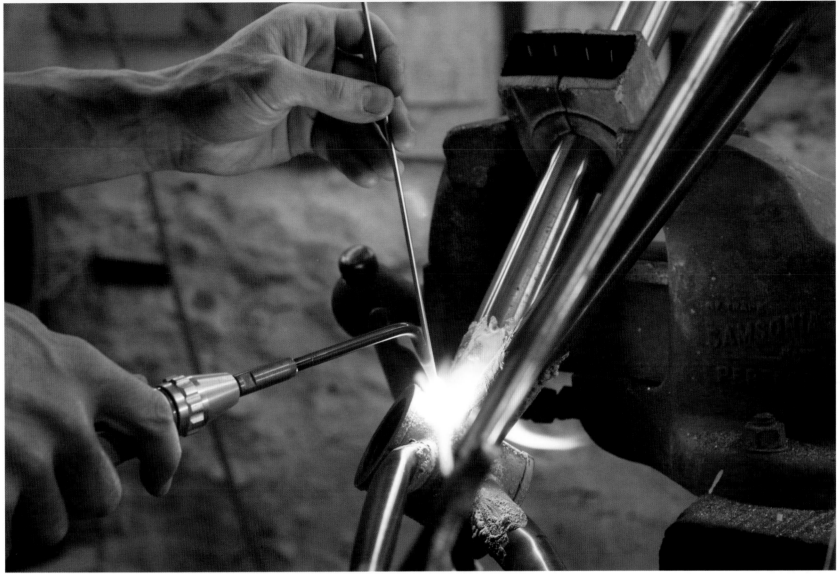

Adding brass fillet to bottom bracket of a single-speed mountain bike

Fillet-brazed stem with captive wedge-style binder, lamp mount, and integrated top cap

650b randonneur bike in Columbus Spirit with Llewellyn Custodian lugs and stainless steel racks

Chrome-plated, fillet-brazed stem with captive wedge-style binder, lamp mount, and integrated top cap

Fixed-gear randonneur bike in Reynolds 725, with Sachs Newvex lugs and custom-made stem and rack

Single-speed mountain bike in Reynolds 853, with Columbus seat stays and fork blades

Signal Cycles

Portland, Oregon, USA

In early 2007, two recent art school graduates and long-time bicycle mechanics began building frames in a small garage in Portland, Oregon. The first few bikes were built using raw but effective tooling, coupled with excitement and energy. Those bikes were built for close friends and kept the garage full of creativity. Realizing their excitement and the growing demand for customized, handbuilt bicycles, Nate Meschke and Matt Cardinal launched Signal Cycles in February 2008. Many things have changed for Signal since then, but at its core, Signal is defined by the partnership of Matt and Nate. The growth of Signal continues to foster creative thinking between the two and has developed Signal into a brand that has a distinctive look and feel.

Bicycles have always been a passion and interest for Matt. From his earliest days of learning the freedom of riding a bike, through his days of BMX and mountain biking, road riding and commuting, bicycles have always been a lifestyle choice. Art and design represent another passion for Matt, and after graduating from art school, Signal allowed him to combine these loves into a dream job of creating beautiful, functional bicycles.

Like most kids, bicycles were important to Nate starting at a very young age. Salvaging old bikes and rebuilding them to satisfy curiosity kept Nate busy until he found his first job as a bike shop kid at the age of 14, sweeping floors. After a few years skiing and biking in Colorado, Nate went to art school, receiving a BFA in painting and design while working a part-time job as a bike mechanic that would turn out to be the start of his adventure in the bicycle industry.

Since the company's start in 2008, Signal has been committed to growing sustainably while pursuing new opportunities. After a very busy first year starting the business, Signal was asked to join the Rapha Continental project in 2009 and built a bike for one of the team members. Sharing Rapha's enduring sense of exploration, Matt and Nate jumped at the opportunity to be involved and created a bike that has been ridden on some of the most epic, off-the-map road rides in North America.

In late 2009, Signal took on a new challenge and began building bikes for their first Signal cyclo-cross team. Portland is known as one of the best cyclo-cross scenes in the world, with more than 1500 racers in 20 different categories racing each Sunday in the fall. Signal asked five talented friends to join the team, with a basic race motto of "fun first, fast second."

In 2011, Signal achieved three great milestones: at the 2011 North American Handbuilt Bike Show they received the award for the "Best City Bike" showing a brushed stainless lugged bike with a small rear rack and generator lighting system; on returning to Portland with the award, Signal signed a lease on a new shop space and quickly moved into the 1000-square-foot shop, purchasing equipment that never would have fit in the garage; and at the same time, Signal was asked to be involved in a collaboration with Ziba, an internationally recognized industrial design firm with offices in Portland, Munich, Tokyo, and Shanghai. The product was to be the ultimate utility bike. Determined to push the design elements while having fun with the project, the team created a modern bike with a detachable side-car, custom-fitted bags and a unique bike-locking mechanism.

At Signal, design, functionality, utility, and aesthetics share an equal spot at the table. Matt and Nate believe every Signal should deliver these elements, creating a bike that is as easy to ride as it is to look at.

"The basic motto of Signal Cycles is 'fun first, speed second'"

"*At Signal, design, functionality, utility, and aesthetics share an equal spot at the table.*"

"The form that is created when a flat dropout is joined with a round tube is beautiful."

Steve Potts Bicycles

Point Reyes, California, USA

Steve Potts's name is synonymous with the early development of mountain bikes and he has been building bikes since 1979. His fondest bike memory is sitting on the handlebars of his older brother's enormous paperboy bike, his brother telling him to hold on tight and get ready to break the sound barrier. When Steve reached the age of 10, he began a paper route of his own and started to explore Mount Tam, which to a 10-year-old was like discovering the entire world. He was the type of kid who relished the outdoors and his bike gave him the freedom to ride all over the mountain to discover creeks and waterfalls and to go fishing.

Many of Steve's skills are the product of growing up with a creative father who made a variety of objects such as telescopes, bows and arrows, musical instruments, and sailplanes. Learning from his father, and being around tools to make and repair all sorts of things, placed Steve in an environment that nurtured his natural talent for designing and building. Like many master frame-builders who have built thousands of bike frames and have expertise in a range of skills, Steve Potts can build a bike from the ground up, and has done so many times.

His technical expertise is such that he is able to design and make everything from the nuts and bolts through to the bike pump, as well as designing the tires and everything in between. Although this would take hours and hours of Steve's time, he would revel in every second of it because he loves nothing more than to work with his hands and use tools and machinery to express a passionate desire to design, solve, and create.

Steve has also made the machinery and tooling equipment for the local family company that casts his head badges. Not surprisingly, the Steve Potts Bicycles head badge features Mount Tam, which was the landscape for his many adventures and a region that has vital links to the development of mountain bikes. Steve Potts was inducted into the Mountain Bike Hall of Fame in 1989 in recognition of his work as one of the early pioneers of mountain trail bikes. In 2012 he won the Best Titanium Construction Award at the North American Handmade Bicycle Show for one of his titanium 29ers.

As a testament to the longevity of a well-crafted handmade bike, one of Steve's fully brazed, steel cross-country mountain bikes was once checked in to his workshop to be restored. It was a bike that he had made 25 years before and it was fascinating for him to view his work again after all that time and to see how the bike had performed.

Steve is a sentimentalist at heart and has kept many objects that he made when he was young and proudly displays anything that his own two sons have made. Steve chooses to build his mountain and road frames from titanium because of its raw beauty, mechanical properties, and non-corrosive qualities; he is also regularly called upon to restore and repair many titanium bikes from around the world. When working with titanium, the surface and environment needs to be super clean, so Steve has an ultrasonic cleaner, which he uses to clean the tubes and parts for building new bikes and restorations. The concept of a throw-away society doesn't exist in Steve Potts's world because he builds bikes that can last a lifetime, and his infectious enthusiasm for being able to make anything with his tools and machinery is only matched by his love of his family and the great outdoors.

Strawberry

Portland, Oregon, USA

It's a big leap from loving everything about cycling to wanting to build bike frames. For Andy Newlands, one catalyst was his love of tools. As a confirmed tool freak, the idea of collecting and using a whole range of wonderful implements to build a machine that he loved to ride was a winning combination. He'd always ridden as a kid, toured a bit, and raced, and regards cycling as the most fun you can have while staying fit.

After completing a civil engineering degree, Andy found himself in Scotland during the 1970 British Commonwealth Games and rode to Edinburgh with a bunch of cyclists. In 1971 he also rode the Tour of California in a Pacific Northwest team. It was during this tour that he spotted a bike frame that really impressed him for its workmanship and the subtle lines of the lugs and described it as being "really pretty." Andy was inspired enough to want to begin setting himself on the path to frame building and used his research time to attend bike shows in Milan and Paris to observe as many bikes as he could. Once he had sourced tools, tubing suppliers, and lugs he was ready to begin his frame-building business.

Although his father kept asking him when he was going to get a real job, Andy remained determined and just kept building steel road- and track-frames.

Now, 40 years on, Andy Newlands is not only a master builder but also a master toolmaker. After being in the business for so long, he's seen many advances, but considers that the bike's geometry isn't that much different. In his opinion, the most significant changes have been in steel production, which is now air-hardened so it gains strength at the joint. "You braze it up around 1,500 degrees or so, and the structure is enhanced—it is actually harder and stronger at the join when it's heated to over 1,500–1,600 degrees."

When it came to choosing a name for his business, Andy chose a derivative from a family name to create the name Strawberry. After visiting many bike shops in England in 1970 that were named after the owner, Andy wanted to come up with something that had a touch of humor. His grandmother was a Fraser, which comes from the French word *fraise*, meaning strawberry, so he settled on that for his company name. Andy's workspace is an old motor mechanic's garage that was built in 1948, and here he's surrounded by 2,600 square feet of tools and machinery in all shapes and sizes. While he's working, Andy likes to have music playing and confesses to knowing every Rolling Stones song ever written. As one of his friends often jokingly comments when he visits his workshop: "It's either the Rolling Stones or John Coltrane, get a life." Andy knows he has a great life—he's doing something he loves, is surrounded by a garage full of tools for his trade, and still gets out to ride for enjoyment and occasionally competes in time trials.

"You braze it up around 1,500 degrees or so, and the structure is enhanced—it's actually harder and stronger at the join when it's heated to over 1,500–1,600 degrees."

Light and tight going up ...

"A Strawberry makes it to the Col de l'Iseran, in the French Alps, September 2005. Jim Draudt, Rob Witsil, and Dave Worthington made this the highest point of many highs during a week riding through the Alps. The Strawberry was fantastic, light and tight going up and rock solid going down."

Jim Draudt, Portland, Oregon

Sweetpea Bicycles

Portland, Oregon, USA

The most distinctive feature of a Sweetpea is the relationship between the bikes and the women who ride them. Everything from the customized geometry to the personal aesthetic choices and features make these bikes intimate personal artifacts. Sweetpea started as the husband-and-wife team of Natalie and Austin Ramsland, but over the last few years has grown into a neat little team of people and partners that help to put more Sweetpeas into the world. At their fit and design studio, Natalie works with both Sweetpea customers and the general public, providing a range of bike-fitting services. An Oregon frame fabricator works closely with her to build the standard and custom geometries of the Lust Line bike models they sell. Jude Kirstein of Sugar Wheel Works provides her with all of custom and handbuilt wheels. She has a wonderful mechanic assembling bikes and even making house calls to her customers.

"When I started building bikes, I didn't have a background in metal fabrication; I didn't have experience as a bike mechanic, nor I didn't have any likely-seeming pre-requisites for the craft. I was working as a bike messenger (again), having recently dropped out of architecture school. I had learned that I loved design work, but was ambivalent about the professional culture of architecture. Riding in Portland, I began to notice how many strong female cyclists I rode with were riding on bikes that didn't fit them well and didn't do justice to their love of cycling. That's when I realized that I could combine my passions for bikes and for design as a bike-builder, by making bikes for women," says Natalie.

The most distinctive feature of a Sweetpea is often invisible. What distinguishes Natalie's bikes from other custom-frames is the way the bikes fit their riders. Her design process begins with a close investigation of the relationship between a frame and an individual, how the frame supports a woman's ideal riding position, with all of her unique quirks and strengths. While Natalie loves beautiful paint jobs, custom racks, and nifty details as much as the next builder, she feels that the carefully considered fit of the bike is the greatest opportunity she has to make a bike feel like an extension of the rider's body.

"I like building with steel because it is a lively, durable material. Because I am focused intently on the fit of the bike, I tend to filet-braze rather than build with lugs, so that my designs are not constrained by the angles in which lugs are manufactured. I also love bar tape and grips. They show wear and express how the bike is ridden and cared for. Sometimes dishevelled, sometimes immaculate, they always bear the evidence of use. When you fall in love with a bike, you want it to be a long-term relationship. A well-crafted steel frame may traverse many continents, many wheel sets, and many decades of use."

The fabrication shop is tucked away in Natalie's backyard and is reflective of the exuberance (and messiness) of making things. She has a large chalkboard wall that captures notes and drawings of work in progress, a cozy perch by her Wilton vise with a view to the chicken coop, and a rolling jig that always seems to be in the path of my dog's favoured lounging spots. Sweetpea shares a retail location with Sugar Wheel Works on a busy bike thoroughfare in northeast Portland. Natalie occupies a small mezzanine over the wheel shop that is private and close enough for some lively banter.

"I fit my customers with a biomechanical approach that addresses strength, flexibility, muscle memory, and any physical limitations as I work with their body on an adjustable bike to find their ideal riding position. I believe that all riders can benefit from a professional bike-fitting, but that women benefit disproportionately because most bikes are still designed and made with a male cyclist in mind. For a lot of my customers, their Sweetpea is the first bike that ever fit them well. I love the magic of brazing the front triangle. Once I tack the front triangle and pull it out of the jig, it already hints at its unique relationship to a body."

When she is alone in her fabrication shop, Natalie loves listening to books on tape and looks forward to even the pickiest of finish work when she has a great story to immerse herself in. She also enjoys singing loudly when the power tools are running, particularly Johnny Cash numbers.

"I love bar tape and grips. They show wear and express how the bike is ridden and cared for. Sometimes dishevelled, sometimes immaculate, they always bear the evidence of use."

Vanilla Bicycles

Portland, Oregon, USA

Located in an old milking parlor of Portland's Belmont Dairy building, the understated Vanilla signage welcomes people who have sought the firm out, without attracting too much attention from the general public. Customers are often first drawn to Vanilla Bicycles for their aesthetic qualities, from the color palettes to the use of raw metal to complement painted portions, right down to the overall shape of the bike being balanced and "right." After the initial connection with the aesthetics, the unique qualities of a Vanilla bike can be found below the surface, where many of the aesthetic, sexy touches also have purpose. It is this level of detail that allows the customer to form a close relationship with their Vanilla.

The creator and owner of Vanilla Bicycles, Sacha White, is driven by the challenge to do better today than he did yesterday. This philosophy extends from craftsmanship to design and business, through to taking good care of his clients. "I always try to improve on what I've done before. Each new bike or concept stands on the shoulders of what I have done in the past and what my mentors have done before me." Sacha stands by the adage that there

is potential for greatness everywhere we look and is a firm believer that it's not the material or method of construction used, but what the builder does with his given materials.

Sacha's choice of material is steel because it is what he started working with and is the medium with which he refined his bike-building skills. He's the sole builder at Vanilla and is fortunate to have a handful of great people who take care of the peripheral tasks. His role at Vanilla includes being the fit-specialist, designer, and frame builder, while Scott, his assistant, preps the frames for paint and polishes stainless steel, and also takes care of packing and shipping, customer service, parts ordering, and bike builds.

The Vanilla workspace is also a reflection of the way Sacha White likes to conduct his business: "It has always been important to me that when someone comes to visit Vanilla, they are welcomed into a beautiful space—a space that really represents Vanilla's world." Inside, the customer enters a refined, but rustic environment where they can view Vanilla bicycles in the boutique showroom.

For the measuring process there is a dedicated private fitting area and a separate design and office space to discuss ideas. The workshop section at the rear of the building is where all the metal fabrication takes place.

Sacha has been creating Vanilla bicycles for more than 10 years and has found that the subtle nuances of construction and alignment always hold an opportunity for improvement. He enjoys dissecting his projects and putting the pieces back together to create something more ideal. One feature that he is particularly proud of is the integrated braking system of the Speedvagen Cyclocross bikes because it's a feature that he's never seen on another bike and believes that it is a real improvement on the traditional system. Sacha rides bikes as a form of transport to get both himself and his family around, and also likes to race cyclocross and ride with friends and the Vanilla team. When he's not spending time with his family, creating bikes or cycling, you can be sure that Sacha is taking time out to dream of new projects.

"It has always been important to me that when someone comes to visit Vanilla, they are welcomed into a beautiful space—a space that really represents Vanilla's world."

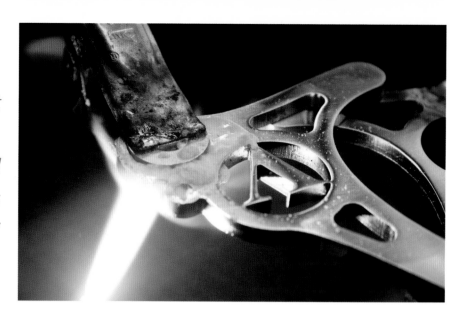

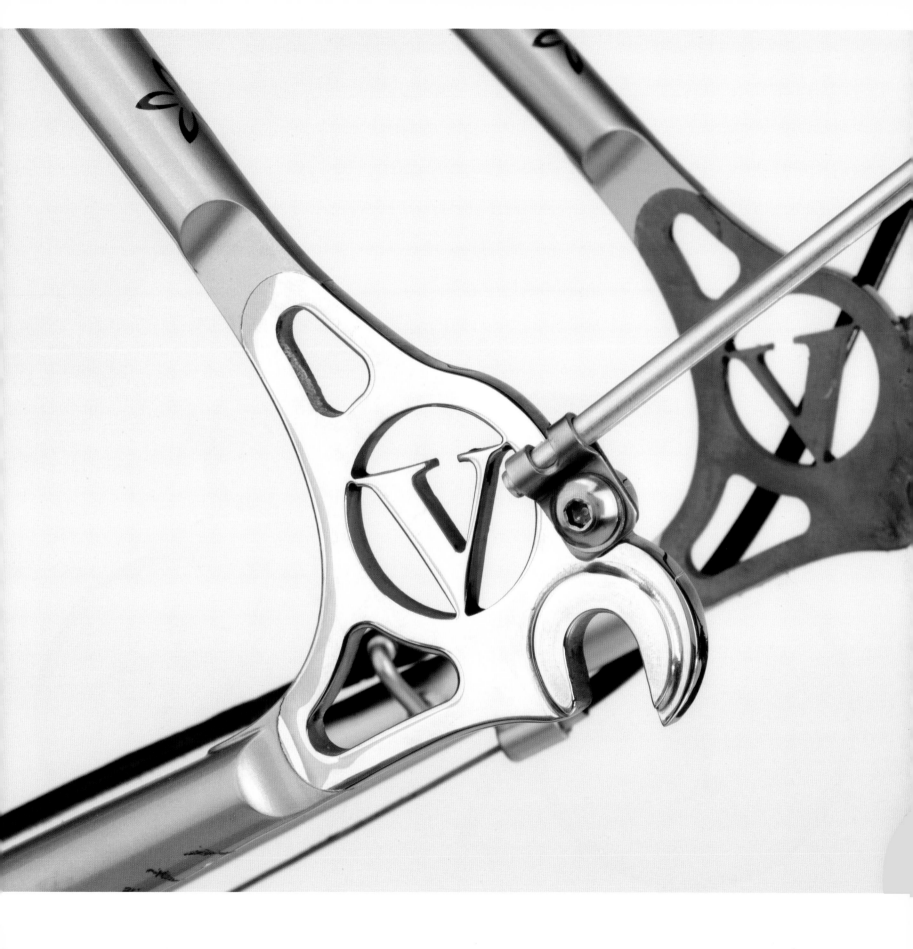

"I always try to improve on what I've done before. Each new bike or concept stands on the shoulders of what I have done in the past and what my mentors have done before me."

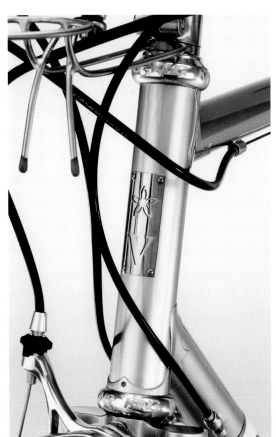

Vendetta Cycles

Willamette Valley, Oregon, USA

Vendetta Cycles is very much about two guys making beautiful objects that make people smile. A combination of degrees in mechanical engineering and metallurgy along with an acetylene torch, found Conor Buescher and Garrett Clark establishing a business in 2004. Building custom bicycles allowed them to combine engineering know-how, practical experience, and dedication to the craftsmanship of lugged-steel bikes. Conor had many years experience riding, racing, and selling bikes, whereas Garrett's interests had been in all things mechanical and the hobby of motor racing. Conor and Garrett are thoroughly dedicated to building lugged bikes and believe the real spirit of the bicycle is seen in the lugs, which are the confluence of the three most important features of Vendetta bikes—function, craftsmanship, and beauty.

In terms of functionality, lugs provide structural reinforcement in the most heavily stressed part of the bike. Craftsmanship is expressed in the edges of the lugs, where brazed shorelines should be crisp and smooth, because they show the skill of the constructor. And for sheer beauty, the pointy shape of the lugs is intended primarily to smooth the structural transition from the lug to the tube, and this goal can be met with an infinite variety of artfully designed shapes. Their devotion to lugs is equaled by an enthusiasm for building with steel, which perfectly matches their design philosophy because of its high strength and excellent formability. It also allows for thin tube walls that ensure a lightweight bicycle with excellent riding characteristics. Steel is also compatible with their preferred joining technique of silver-brazing and lugged construction.

Conor and Garrett confer on every aspect of each frame design and construction. They are so committed to this approach that both must approve every part of the design, construction, and finish work. It makes for very vibrant discussions and critical analysis of every decision, but they also have their areas of expertise. "I think you can say we have a lot of fun at work, and that simultaneously respectful and irreverent attitude can be seen in the unique quality of our work." Classic rock of the 1960s and '70s such as Led Zeppelin can be heard as a backdrop to their lively debates, although they sometimes stretch to the '90s with some Pacific Northwest grunge rock and more modern British Blues sounds.

The entire building process has many great moments for them both: "Once the lug carving is complete, the true soul of the bike is identifiable. Once the major tubes have been joined, the complete structure is visible. When the polishing and paint are done the feeling is not unlike a birthday." Their favorite part of the process is definitely the reaction from the bike's new owner, when they say something like: "I can tell you put a lot of love into building this bike. The ride is sublime. You've outdone yourselves."

It isn't just owners of the bikes who are raving about their work. Vendetta Cycles won the award for Best Finish at the 2012 North American Handmade Bicycle Show in Sacramento, California. While awards are appreciated, Conor and Garrett continue to build bicycles to satisfy an inner desire to create something unique, functional, and beautiful.

The bike sings ...

"The bike rides like a dream, super smooth and stable at every speed. I've taken her out on numerous club rides, you know the kind, where all the carbon and titanium frames come out to play. Everybody is blown away by the beauty and handmade craftsmanship. The fork whistles in the pitch of d# at the right speed, so I guess the bike sings."

Gary Schmid

"Once the lug carving is complete, the true soul of the bike is identifiable. Once the major tubes have been joined, the complete structure is visible. When the polishing and paint are done the feeling is not unlike a birthday."

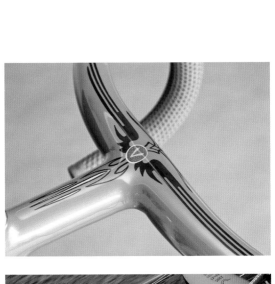

Vicious Cycles

New Paltz, New York, USA

Carl Schlemowitz believes that there's a moment in time for some people when cycling transcends sport and becomes a lifestyle. It begins to permeate all areas of their life and they tend to live and breathe everything cycling-related: these are the kind of clients who are attracted to owning a custom-made bicycle from Vicious Cycles.

For Carl, cycling is a simple and fun thing to do, but importantly it is also emotionally and spiritually fulfilling: "Some people say it's kind of like meditating when they're out for a ride." When it came to choosing a name for his company over 18

years ago, Carl Schlemowitz chose Vicious Cycles because of the potential for multiple interpretations. He liked the idea that a bike has the ability to take people away from whatever vicious cycle may be pushing them down in life. Alternatively, it could also refer to the aggression needed by a rider and their bike to navigate over bumpy mountain biking terrains.

Carl feels that cycling is more than just fun—it is also a very liberating experience. He believes that riding offers people a sense of freedom and appreciates the historical link that bicycles have with the women's suffrage movement. The bicycle became a symbol of liberation for many women fighting for the right to vote, and a large number of women gained a certain sense of independence by taking up riding as a form of transport.

When building a bike for a customer, the passion that Carl and his team have for cycling extends through

to the creative construction and finishing touches. From an artistic background, Carl was keen to use his creativity in the design and construction of his bikes, which are also widely admired for their innovative and high-quality paint designs. Vicious Cycles can turn a simple bike frame into a traveling piece of art. Carl is also dedicated to continually testing new technological developments and striving to improve Vicious Cycles' bike designs and processes.

The Vicious Cycles team produces a range of steel and titanium bikes, including road, touring, mountain, fat tire, and cyclocross, all of which are made by hand at the Vicious Cycles workshop. Customers often ask about the dog on the head badge. It is a likeness of Shayla, Carl's Alaskan Husky, who was just a puppy when Carl established Vicious Cycles. He decided that her image would make a good head badge for his bikes, and her likeness has been included on every bicycle that Vicious Cycles has produced. Shayla passed away just shy of 15 years old but she lives on in spirit as an icon of Vicious Cycles.

"Some people say it's kind of like meditating when they're out for a ride."

Wolfhound Cycles

Talent, Oregon, USA

After graduating from college with a health promotions degree in 1998, Fred Cuthbert struggled to find a vocation that would keep him creatively satisfied and also physically active. It was a developing love for mountain biking that would eventually lead him to building bikes. Fred was drawn to the process of designing and creating custom bicycles because it enabled him to work as both craftsman and artist, combining mechanical functionality with art in design.

When Fred started building bikes in 2001, he owned a Wolfhound called Duncan. Fred not only thought that this provided the perfect name for his business, but he also decided to design the Wolfhound head badge in the dog's likeness. Sadly, Duncan has since passed away, but Fred has another Wolfhound who is carrying on the tradition. Fred's workspace is a cargo trailer with a tall roof, located in his backyard. Once he enters his "box" each morning, the music is the first thing that is turned on, which is another passion in his life.

When it comes to custom-made bikes, Fred believes that no-one should ever buy such a specialized and expensive piece of equipment as his or her first bike. Therefore, most of his customers are experienced riders who come to him already knowing exactly what they want in a bike, and in some cases have already pre-prepared all their measurements. Fred considers it important to evaluate each client's current bike and engages his customers with a thorough consultation to discover their preferred riding characteristics and style. Many customers are seriously involved in cycling and are often seeking extremely specific elements in their custom bikes.

Fred believes that most people appreciate and understand the time that goes into designing and building a custom bike because they are just as passionate about their riding as he is about his building: "To me, the process of building a bike is indeed an art, and nothing exemplifies this art more than a beautifully brazed bike." Fred considers it

a huge compliment to be able to build someone the primary machine for what is usually his or her greatest passion. Sometimes the wait list for a Wolfhound bike can be several months, but for Fred, finding people that don't mind waiting is actually an inspiring thing. His clients want a bike with individuality, to have a point of difference, and to know that the bike has been specifically fitted and made for them alone. Fred Cuthbert feels incredibly fortunate to be able to pursue his passion for bicycles, because he can't imagine doing anything else.

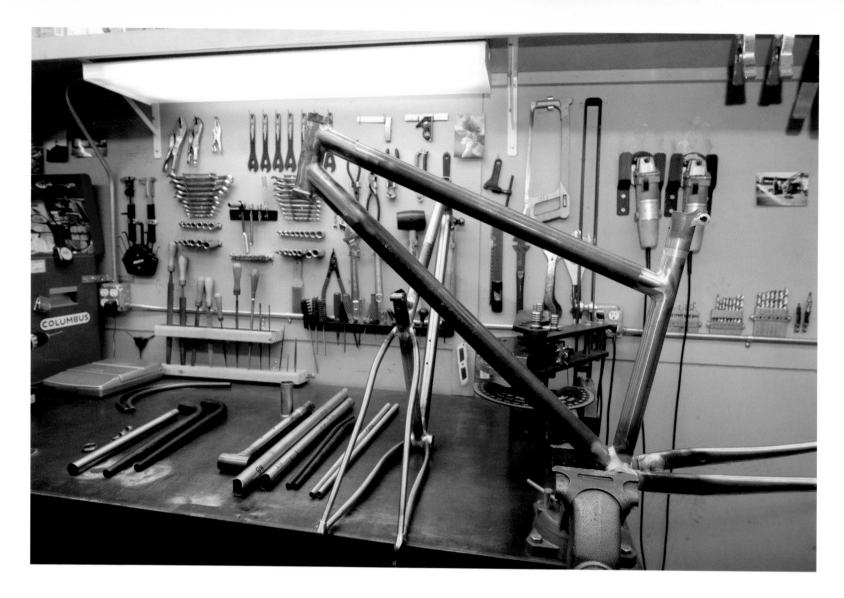

"To me, the process of building a bike is indeed an art, and nothing exemplifies this art more than a beautifully brazed bike."

I was at home with this bike...

"Got the chance to ride this bike today...It's a beautiful work of art with flowing and purposeful tubes, but its stance says "let's rip some trail!" I've been riding a 5"29er for the last few years and my appetite for speed has increased—just rolling through and over everything. On a rigid and foreign bike I'd certainly be taking it down a notch, right? Not a chance.

I was at home with this bike. The trails were as good as it gets and so was this bike—so nimble. These are 29 wheels? I could flick the rear and the front was light for wheelies and manuals. And fast. Absolutely brilliant, Fred. Thank you for an inspiring ride. Sign me up!"

Michael Vose

Contact details

Anderson Custom Bicycles
www.andersoncustombicycles.com

Baum Cycles
www.baumcycles.com

Bilenky Cycle Works
www.bilenky.com

Black Sheep Bikes
www.blacksheepbikes.com

Bob Brown Cycles
www.bobbrowncycles.com

Bohemian Bicycles
www.bohemianbicycles.com

Bruce Gordon Cycles
www.bgcycles.com

Calfee Design
www.calfeedesign.com

Columbine Cycle Works
www.columbinecycle.com

Crisp Titanium
www.crisptitanium.com

Cycles Alex Singer
www.cycles-alex-singer.fr

Cyfac
www.cyfac.fr

Davidson Handbuilt Bicycles
www.davidsonbicycles.com

Don Walker Cycles
www.donwalkercycles.com

Donhou Bicycles
www.donhoubicycles.com

GURU Bikes
www.gurubikes.com

Independent Fabrication
www.ifbikes.com

Ira Ryan Cycles
www.iraryancycles.com

Jeff Jones Custom Bicycles
www.jonesbikes.com

Keith Anderson Cycles
www.keithandersoncycles.com

Kirk Frameworks
www.kirkframeworks.com

Kish Fabrication
www.kishbike.com

Llewellyn Custom Bicycles
www.llewellynbikes.com

Lynskey Performance Designs
www.lynskeyperformance.com

Marschall Framework
www.marschall-framework.de

Moots
www.moots.com

Naked Bicycles and Design
www.timetogetnaked.com

Pegoretti
www.pegoretticicli.com

Richard Sachs Cycles
www.richardsachs.com

Roark Custom Titanium Bicycles
www.roarkcycles.com

Robin Mather
www.robinmathercycles.co.uk

Signal Cycles
www.signalcycles.com

Steve Potts Bicycles
www.stevepottsbicycles.com

Strawberry
www.strawberrybicycle.com

Sweetpea Bicycles
www.sweetpeabicycles.com

Vanilla Bicycles
www.vanillabicycles.com

Vendetta Cycles
www.vendettacycles.com

Vicious Cycles
www.viciouscycles.com

Wolfhound Cycles
www.wolfhoundcycles.com

Photography credits

Introduction

Page 7: David Jablonka

Page 8: Nate Armbrust

Page 9: Craig Mole, courtesy Brett Horton

Page 10 (top left): Robin Mather

Page 10 (top right and bottom): courtesy Calfee Design

Page 11 (top): Dean Bentley

Page 11 (bottom): courtesy Vendetta Cycles

Anderson Custom Bicycles

All images: courtesy Anderson Custom Bicycles

Baum Cycles

Page 17, 19, 20 (top): Jim Hsu

Pages 18 (top left and top right), 20 (bottom left and bottom right), 21, 22 Robert Zappulla

Pages 18 (bottom left and bottom right), 23: courtesy Baum Cycles

Bilenky Cycle Works

Pages 25, 26 (left): courtesy Bilenky Cycle Works

Page 26 (right): Jack Ramsdale

Page 27 (top left and top right): Ken Toda

Page 27 (bottom left): Matt Ramano

Page 27 (bottom right): Allan Rodzinski

Black Sheep Bikes

All images: courtesy Black Sheep Bikes

Bob Brown Cycles

All images: Bob Brown

Bohemian Bicycles

Pages 39, 41 (bottom): Kathi Moore

Page 40: Nick Jensen

Page 41 (top): courtesy Bohemian Bicycles

Bruce Gordon Cycles

All images: Matthew Farruggio

Calfee Design

Page 49, 51, 52, 53, 54, 55: courtesy Calfee Design

Page 50: Paul Schraub

Columbine Cycle Works

Pages 57, 59 (left): Brian McDivitt Photography

Pages 58, 59 (top right and bottom right): Milt Borchert

Crisp Titanium

Pages 61, 62 (bottom), 63 (top left, top right): Gabriele Galimberti

Pages 62 (top), 63 (bottom left) 64, 65: courtesy Crisp Titanium

Page 63 (bottom right): ORME.TV

Cycles Alex Singer

Pages 67, 69 (top right): Jean-Pierre Praderes

Page 68, 69 (top left, bottom): courtesy Cycles Alex Singer

Cyfac

Page 71: Kevin Saunders

Pages 72, 74 (top left): Daniel Pickering

Page 73: courtesy Cyfac

Page 74 (top right, middle right): Eric Sakalowsky

Page 74 (bottom left): Pierre Bonnet

Page 75: Matthew McKee

Davidson Handbuilt Bicycles

All images: Bill Davidson

Donhou Bicycles

Page 81: Andi Sapey

Pages 82, 83: courtesy Donhou Bicycles

Pages 84, 85: Hal Shinnie

Don Walker Cycles

Page 87: Mark Dawson

Pages 88, 89, 90, 91: Joe Vondersaar

GURU Bikes

Pages 93, 95 (bottom right), 96, 97: Studio Pettas

Pages 94, 95 (top left, top right, bottom left): Maurice Richichi

Independent Fabrication

All images: courtesy Independent Fabrication

Ira Ryan Cycles

All photos: courtesy Ira Ryan Cycles

Jeff Jones Custom Bicycles

Pages 111, 112 (top left), 113, 114: Tim Tidball

Pages 112 (top right), 115, 116, 117 (left and top right): Jeff Jones

Page 112 (bottom): Korbin Jones

Page 117 (bottom right): Jonathan Bacon

Keith Anderson Cycles

All images: Keith Anderson

Kirk Frameworks

All images: David Kirk; except page 124 (bottom right) Karin Kirk

Kish Fabrication

All images: Colin Michael Photography

Llewellyn Custom Bicycles

All images: Journey of Life Photography

Lynskey Performance Designs

Pages 141, 142 (top), 143 (bottom), 144, 145: Matt Richardson

Page 142 (bottom): Ed Ibbetson

Page 143 (top): Cedric Parys

Marschall Framework

All images: Klaus Schneider

Moots

Pages 153, 154, 155 (bottom right, bottom left), 157 (bottom left): Michael Robson

Page 155 (top): Dave Epperson

Page 156, 157 (top, bottom right): Jamie Kripke

Naked Bicycles and Design

All images: courtesy Naked Bicycles and Design

Pegoretti

Pages 163, 164 (bottom), 165, 166, 167, 169: Herman Seidl Tirez

Page 164 (top left, top center, top right): courtesy Pegoretti

Page 168: Gita Sporting Goods Ltd

Richard Sachs Cycles

Pages 171, 173 (bottom right), 174, 175: Jeff Weir Photography

Page 172 (top): Eric Carlson Photography

Page 172 (bottom left): Anthony Skorochod

Page 172 (bottom right): Richard Sachs

Page 173 (top and bottom left): Michael Edwards Photography

Roark Custom Titanium Bicycles

Pages 181, 184, 185: Brad Quartuccio

Pages 182, 183: Farid A. Abraham

Robin Mather

All images: Robin Mather

Signal Cycles

Pages 191, 192, 193, 194, 195: Matt Cardinal

Pages 196, 197: Ziba

Steve Potts Bicycles

Pages 199, 200 (left and top right), 203 (top), 204, 205 (top right): Dean Bentley

Pages 200 (bottom right), 201 (top right): Steve Potts

Pages 201 (bottom), 202, 203 (bottom left and bottom right), 205 (bottom right): Stuart Schwartz

Strawberry

Page 207: Joe Hawes, Flash Pro

Page 208 (bottom): David Jablonka

Pages 208 (top), 209: Andy Newlands

Sweetpea Bicycles

All images: courtesy Sweetpea Bicycles

Vanilla Bicycles

Pages 215, 218, 219: Craig Mole, courtesy Brett Horton

Pages 216, 217: Robert M. Huff

Vendetta Cycles

Pages 221, 222 (top right and top left), 223 (bottom left): courtesy Vendetta Cycles

Pages 222 (bottom), 223 (middle left): Tina Buescher Photography

Page 223 (right): Jonathan Maus

Vicious Cycles

Page 225: Sean Davis

Page 226: Craig Harrison

Page 227: courtesy Vicious Cycles

Wolfhound Cycles

All images: Sean Bagshaw; except page 230 Jason Van Horn Photography

Acknowledgments

We would like to thank all the wonderfully talented bike builders who have contributed to the revised edition of this book. They continue to build custom bicycles in their own unique way and provide many bike enthusiasts with the glorious dilemma of which bike to choose.

A special thank you to Paul Latham and Alessina Brooks from the Images Publishing Group for having the vision to publish a revised edition of the book in recognition of bicycle builders as artisans and the huge interest in bicycles and cycling around the world. A big thank you also goes to the editor, Driss Fatih, for his support in putting this edition together.

Christine Elliott and David Jablonka